MW01613525

Category Management Antitrust Handbook

SECTION OF
ANTITRUST LAW

**Defending Liberty
Pursuing Justice**

This volume should be officially cited as:

ABA SECTION OF ANTITRUST LAW,
CATEGORY MANAGEMENT ANTITRUST HANDBOOK (2010)

CONTENTS

FOREWORD

The Section of Antitrust Law is pleased to present the *Category Management Antitrust Handbook*. The *Handbook* is intended to explain how category management works from a business standpoint and then to address the economic and legal issues which can arise. The book is directed to a non-legal as well as legal audience.

The Section is indebted to those who contributed to this *Handbook*. This was a joint project of the Unilateral Conduct Committee and the Civil Enforcement Committee. The *Handbook* would not have been possible without the dedication and hard work of its project chairs, editors, and authors, especially Gregory Huffman, Jay Levine, Julie Soloway, and Albert Kim who guided the publication through to completion.

October 2010

Allan Van Fleet
Chair, Section of Antitrust Law
American Bar Association
2010–2011

PREFACE

Category management is a relatively new development in retailing in which the retailer works closely with one or more major suppliers in making and implementing decisions which affect an entire category of products. Because suppliers can become involved in the retailer's decisions affecting their competitors' products, courts and commentators have focused on the antitrust implications of the category management process. The development of category management has paralleled the growth of large national chain retailers, the computerization of consumer sales, and the increasing presence of private label brands owned by retailers. This *Handbook* addresses that confluence of events, with the purpose of identifying and explaining the business, economic, and legal issues raised from an antitrust perspective by category management.

The Section is indebted to those who contributed to this *Handbook*. This was a joint project of the Unilateral Conduct Committee and the Civil Enforcement Committee. Many individuals contributed. The chapters were authored by Gregory Huffman, Timothy Daniel, Jeffrey Berhold, Kenneth Field, Theodore Banks, and Amanda Wait. The book was edited by Gregory Huffman, Jay Levine, Joyce Bartoo, Albert Kim, James Musgrove, Robin Moore, Jonathan Jacobson, Debra Pearlstein, Alicia Downey, Josh Wright, Max Huffman, Sean Gates, and Brian Stoltz. Others assisting included Julie Soloway, Kenneth Glazer, Arthur Lerner, Robert Skitol, Daniel Savrin, Jen Driscoll, Maria DiMoscato, and Joan Heim.

We hope this book provides helpful guidance to those in the retailing business and their legal counsel.

October 2010

Patricia Brink
Chair, Unilateral Conduct Committee

Anthony W. Swisher
Chair, Unilateral Conduct Committee
Section of Antitrust Law
American Bar Association
2010–11

INTRODUCTION

"Category management" is a relatively new concept that has become ubiquitous in some segments of the retailing industry. When a retailer engages in category management, it often designates a principal supplier in a particular product category as a "category captain" to help the retailer make decisions maximizing profits across all suppliers' products in that category. This practice has become widespread in the marketing of consumer goods.

Category management has been the focus of at least two high-profile private antitrust lawsuits.[1] The FTC devoted a chapter of its 2001 report on slotting allowances to the subject.[2] The agency has also conducted investigations into the manner in which several large grocery suppliers have dealt with retailers in the context of a category-management relationship.[3] More recently, the FTC reportedly has opened an ongoing investigation into the potentially anticompetitive use of category captains in the retail sale of condoms.[4] In other countries, the antitrust authorities have addressed category management in some of their guidelines.[5]

---

1. Conwood Co. v. United States Tobacco Co., 290 F.3d 768 (6th Cir. 2002); El Aguila Food Prods. v. Gruma Corp., 301 F. Supp. 2d 612 (S.D. Tex. 2003), aff'd, 131 F. App'x 450 (5th Cir. 2005).

2. Fed. Trade Comm'n, REPORT ON THE FEDERAL TRADE COMMISSION WORKSHOP ON SLOTTING ALLOWANCES AND OTHER MARKETING PRACTICES IN THE GROCERY INDUSTRY (2001), available at http://www.ftc.gov/os/2001/02/slottingallowancesreportfinal.pdf.

3. See, e.g., Fed. Trade Comm'n, Analysis of Agreement Containing Consent Orders to Aid Public Comment, In the Matter of the Procter & Gamble Company and the Gillette Company, File No. 051-0115 (Sept. 30, 2005), available at http://www.ftc.gov/os/caselist/0510115/050930ana0510115.pdf.

4. See Condom Category Captain Case, 741 FTC WATCH 1, 1-3 (May 4, 2009). The investigation centers on Trojan condoms, the largest selling brand of condoms in the United States. Id. at 3. The manufacturer, Church & Dwight, reported in its May 2010 quarterly report that it has received a subpoena and civil investigative demand and that the FTC is

This publication is an attempt to provide businesspeople and legal practitioners with a better understanding of the economic and legal frameworks used to analyze category management. By way of background, Chapter I lays out how category management works as a business concept in a retailing environment. Chapter II identifies the economic issues that can arise from the category management practice of appointing a supplier as a category captain with responsibility for advising the retailer as to selection, display, promotion, and even pricing decisions. Finally, Chapter III examines the potential antitrust risks in the use of category captains, summarizes agency views of related retail practices, and offers practical suggestions for mitigating risk.

"seeking to determine if [Church & Dwight] has engaged in or is engaging in any unfair methods of competition with respect to the distribution and sale of condoms in the United States through potentially exclusionary practices." Church & Dwight Co., Quarterly Report (10-Q), at 16 (May 11, 2010).

5.   *See, e.g.,* Israel Antitrust Authority, Stance of the General Director on Commercial Arrangements between Food Suppliers and Retail Chains (Jan. 5, 2005), *available at* http://eng-archive.antitrust.gov.il/files/52/Retail%20Chains.pdf; Canada Competition Bureau, The Abuse of Dominance Provisions (Sections 78 and 79 of the *Competition Act*) as Applied to the Canadian Grocery Sector (November 2002), *available at* http://strategis.ic.gc.ca/pics/ct/ct02465e.pdf.

CHAPTER I

CATEGORY MANAGEMENT AND CATEGORY CAPTAINCY: HOW THEY FUNCTION

Category management emerged as a retail management philosophy in the 1990s. Rather than the retailer negotiating the best deal with each supplier and relying on consumers to sort between the brands, some retailers began planning in advance for an entire category of products. Some consumers like a well-known brand even if it costs more; other consumers want a lower-price product; other consumers are moved more by a product's natural or higher quality ingredients, unusual designs or formulations, or color. Retailers increasingly chose to differentiate between products of the same type, based on the different consumer response each product in a category generates. Some retailers also have made a greater effort to stock their own brands ("house brands" or "private labels"). With the advent of computerized databases and scanned product bar codes, retailers have huge amounts of information about consumer purchases available on a daily basis. All of these factors have become a part of the concept called category management.

An important aspect of category management is reliance on one or more suppliers to inform the retailer about what is happening in the development and manufacture of a product category and to assist the retailer in making decisions about that category. Those decisions include which products to stock, how to display them, how to promote and advertise them, and even how to price them to the consumer. The supplier the retailer chooses for this assistance is sometimes referred to as a category captain or an aisle captain.

None of these developments is really new; each is an extension of a traditional retail practice. Suppliers have always bent the ears of shopkeepers, and shopkeepers have often relied on suppliers' advice and comments. Shopkeepers have tried to understand what consumers want and to stock the mix of products which will maximize profit. What is new is that these practices have been made part of a formal management philosophy called "category management," this philosophy seems to be increasing in popularity, a supplier is often given an influential role in decision making, and some believe that that role may have negative implications for competition.

A. The Complexity of Retailing

Many retail stores carry thousands of different types of products, or Stock Keeping Units (SKUs). Over the last several decades, retail stores have tended to increase in size and can cover in excess of 100,000 square feet (more than three football fields).[1] As store size has increased, so has the size and complexity of store inventory.[2]

Managing the inventory of a modern retail store is not an easy job. Each type of product is usually available from a number of different suppliers, in varying colors, types, and package sizes. Each color, type, and package size of each supplier's product is a separate SKU, and there may be tens of thousands of SKUs vying for a place in a retailer's inventory.[3] Each year suppliers offer new products and new SKUs; in the grocery business, approximately 24,000 products are introduced each year.[4] Failure rates for new grocery products have been estimated to range up to 80 percent.[5]

A retailer needs to decide which SKUs to stock, where in the store to display each SKU, how much shelf space to commit to that SKU, what price to charge for the SKU, and in what advertising and promotional activities to engage for the SKU. Pricing, promotion, advertising, and

---

1. NIELSEN MKTG. RESEARCH, CATEGORY MANAGEMENT: POSITIONING YOUR ORGANIZATION TO WIN 18 (1992) (showing square footages range from 22,500 for a conventional supermarket, 42,000 for a superstore, and up to 174,000 for a hypermarket).

2. *See id.* (showing the number of items sold ranges from 15,000 for a conventional supermarket to over 100,000 for a hypermarket); Peter Boatwright & Joseph C. Nunes, *Reducing Assortment: An Attribute-Based Approach*, 65 J. MKTG. 50 (2001) (noting that the average number of SKUs in a supermarket has increased to more than 30,000).

3. Norm Borin, Paul W. Farris & James R. Freeland, *A Model for Determining Retail Product Category Assortment and Shelf Space Allocation*, 25 DECISION SCI. 359 (1994) (explaining that chains choose from over 60,000 SKUs); FOOD MARKETING INSTITUTE, SLOTTING ALLOWANCES IN THE SUPERMARKET INDUSTRY 2-3 (2002), http://www.fmi.org/ media/bg/slottingfees2002.pdf (reporting that "about 100,000 grocery products are available on the market").

4. Ronald W. Davis, *A Mystery Wrapped in an Enigma: Slotting Allowances and Antitrust*, 15 ANTITRUST 69 (2001) (estimating that 24,000 new products are introduced yearly, twice as many as ten years before).

5. Food Marketing Institute, *supra* note 3, at 2 ("Depending on how a new product is defined, the failure rate ranges up to 80 percent per year.").

store location for the SKU may change monthly, weekly, or even more often, depending on the store's marketing strategy.

The hundreds of thousands of SKU-specific decisions a retailer makes every year do not occur in a vacuum. In a given store, if shelf space of one SKU is increased, then likely the shelf space for other SKUs must be decreased. If one SKU is placed on an end-of-aisle display or temporary table, that SKU usually displaces another SKU. If a retailer decides to place one SKU on a special sale, the retailer must make a decision as to what changes, if any, should be made in the pricing of other SKUs. If one SKU is placed in a retailer's advertisement, the retailer must make a decision as to what other SKUs are placed in the same advertisement.

Although consumers appreciate having a variety of choices, a retailer's inventory decisions are framed by, among other things, the physical limits of the store. Each store has, at least in the short term, a given amount of floor space. Shelving in the store also tends to be relatively constant over the short term, even if floor displays and temporary tables may change daily.

A store also has delivery limitations, due to the size of its loading dock and the need to avoid disrupting consumer shopping during peak hours. Many grocery retailers will restrict deliveries to certain hours for the latter reason. Suppliers who deliver their product directly to retail stores (known as direct store delivery) must schedule their deliveries in accordance with each store's delivery rules. If a direct store delivery supplier does not have enough shelf space to stock merchandise to satisfy consumer demand between delivery opportunities, the shelf will become empty and both the retailer and supplier will risk losing sales. However, a retailer may be able to accommodate only a limited number of direct store delivery suppliers because of both shelf space and delivery constraints.

In addition to the general issue of whether a product's sales and profitability justify the space given it, shelf space for perishable products presents an additional problem. A perishable product that sits too long on a shelf can become spoiled or stale. If a perishable product has too much shelf space, the inventory items will not turn quickly enough to stay saleable.

B. Category Management as a Process of Retail Management

No single approach is used by retailers in selecting and selling inventory. There are likely as many management approaches as there are retailers. Two processes, however, have been recognized in this area—brand management and category management.

Historically, brand management was used to determine brand-specific pricing, promotion, and advertising offers by each supplier, sometimes with little consideration as to how the offers would affect other products.[6] For example, a retailer might decide which Colgate® toothpaste products to carry, then which Crest® toothpaste products to carry, and so on for other sellers of branded toothpaste.

Brand management is said to date back to the 1870s and to have arisen coincident with the creation of nationally-recognized brands.[7] As a concept, brand management originated with suppliers and formed the basis of the dialogue with retailers as to how the retailer would make its inventory decisions.[8]

Category management arose more than fifteen years ago[9] as a process which "involves managing product categories as individual business units."[10] This new approach was "seen as a backlash to the failure of the brand management approach" of "not seeing the forest for the trees."[11] Category management tends to be more holistic than brand management. Rather than a decision being made looking only at the attractiveness of a supplier's offer for a particular SKU, category management views the decision from the perspective of how that decision will impact the sale of all products and the retailer's overall profitability in the product category. If changing the way a SKU is sold will divert sales away from more profitable SKUs sold by the retailer, the retailer may decide not to make the change. Category management can

---

6.   *See* George S. Low & Ronald A. Fullerton, *Brands, Brand Management and the Brand Manager System*, 31 J. MKTG. RES. 173, 173 (1994) (explaining that brand managers are "production, not consumer, oriented").

7.   *See id.* at 174.

8.   *Id.*

9.   *See* Amanda Berragan, *Category Management Insight: The Love/Hate Relationship*, RETAIL WORLD, July 8, 2002, at 40 (stating that Wal-Mart started using category management in 1992).

10.   NIELSEN MKTG. RESEARCH, *supra* note 1, at 26; *see also* GROCERY MFRS. ASS'N, CATEGORY MANAGEMENT REPORT: ENHANCING CONSUMER VALUE IN THE GROCERY INDUSTRY xix (1995) (category management defined as a "distributor/supplier process of managing categories as strategic business units").

11.   *See* Christian Dussart, *Category Management: Strength, Limits, and Developments,* 16 EUROPEAN MGMT. J. 50, 52-53 (1998).

be seen as a shift in focus from the supplier's perspective to the retailer's perspective.[12]

Category management has gone hand-in-hand with the increasing sophistication of marketing research. An extensive body of research has investigated the range of consumer preferences and incentives. Category management recognizes that different types of shoppers may choose different SKUs of the same product. Brand shoppers will look for well-known brands; price shoppers will look for less expensive alternatives; impulse shoppers will react on the spur of the moment.[13] Although consumers generally value having a varied assortment to consider,[14] in some categories consumers do not consider variety to be important and reductions in variety can increase sales.[15] Consumers also can react

---

12. *See id.* at 53.

13. *See* Geoff Bayley & Clive Nancarrow, *Impulse Purchasing: A Qualitative Exploration of the Phenomenon*, 1 QUALITATIVE MKT. RES. 99 (1998); Danny N. Bellenger, Dan H. Robertson & Elizabeth C. Hirschman, *Impulse Buying Varies by Product*, 18 J. ADVER. RES. 15, 17 (1978) (finding that impulse purchases varied from 27% to 62% by merchandise line); Cathy J. Cobb & Wayne D. Hoyer, *Planned Versus Impulse Purchase Behavior*, 62 J. RETAILING 384, 406-07 (1986) (finding low levels of impulse purchasing as compared to other studies).

14. Sanjay K. Dhar, Stephen J. Hoch & Nanda Kumar, *Effective Category Management Depends on the Role of the Category*, 77 J. RETAILING 165, 165 (2001) (finding that the best performing retailers offer broader product assortments); Edward J. Fox, Alan L. Montgomery & Leonard M. Lodish, *Consumer Shopping and Spending Across Retail Formats*, 77 J. BUS. S25, S53-56 (2004) (finding that household spending is sensitive to differences in retailer format and assortment); Barbara E. Kahn & Brian Wansink, *The Influence of Assortment Structure on Perceived Variety and Consumption Quantities*, 30 J. CONSUMER RES. 519, 519 (2004) (finding that consumption quantities are influenced by perceived variety).

15. Abdelmajid Amine & Sandrine Gadenat, *Efficient Retailer Assortment: A Consumer Choice Evaluation Perspective*, 31 INT'L J. RETAIL & DISTRIB. MGMT. 486, 486 (2003) (explaining that consumers' perceptions of overall store assortment focus on those product classes where a wide variety is expected but not on other classes); Boatwright & Nunes, *supra* note 2, at 50 (finding that a reduction of SKUs tends to increase sales, on average); Susan M. Broniarczyk, Wayne D. Hoyer & Leigh McAlister, *Consumers' Perceptions of the Assortment Offered in a Grocery Category: The Impact of Item Reduction*, 35 J. MKTG. RES. 166, 166-67 (1998) (finding that a reduction of SKUs does not negatively affect consumer assortment perceptions and store choice if only low-preference

differently when various product types are promoted; for example, niche products can have greater price elasticity than staple products.[16] Category management recognizes the variety of consumer preferences and analyzes which selection, placement, pricing, advertising, and promotion decisions for products in a category will maximize the profit, volume, and other targets set by the retailer.

Category management decisions are informed by increasingly robust databases maintained by retailers.[17]   Computers track consumers' purchases of each product each day.   Sophisticated analyses can show whether a change in the availability, price, advertising, or promotion of one product increased or decreased the retailer's profitability or volume in the entire category.   Commentators and researchers have proposed models to rationalize these decisions since at least the 1980s.[18]   The retailer's goals, logically, are to draw customers from other stores, generate additional purchases from existing customers, or generate sales of higher margin SKUs, rather than just change which equally profitable SKU is chosen by an existing customer.

Developments in retailing also have spurred the use of category management techniques. As retailers have increased the sale of private

---

items are eliminated and category space is held constant); Dhar et al., *supra* note 14, at 180 (finding that the consumer impact of assortment depends on whether the category is a staple, variety enhancer, niche, or fill-in); Jaehwan Kim, Greg M. Allenby & Peter E. Rossi, *Modeling Consumer Demand for Variety*, 21 MKTG. SCI. 229, 249 (2002) (explaining that a retailer with lower variety tends to compensate consumers in some way such as lower prices).

16.   *See* Dhar et al., *supra* note 14, at 180 (suggesting that "regular price elasticities are low in staples").

17.   *See generally* GROCERY MFRS. ASS'N, *supra* note 10, at ch. 6.

18.   Alain Bultez & Philippe Naert, *S.H.A.R.P.:   Shelf Allocation for Retailers' Profit*, 7 MKTG. SCI. 211, 211 (1988) (suggesting a shelf space allocation model and testing it in Belgian chains); Francis Buttle, *Retail Space Allocation*, 14 INT'L J. PHYSICAL DISTRIB. & MATERIALS MGMT. 3 (1984) (discussing principles of retail space allocation in light of the trend to self-service, fewer outlets, pressure on retail margins, and the drift away from planned purchases; retail space allocation looks to fixture location, product category location, item location within categories, off-shelf display and point-of-sale promotional support); Marcel Corstjens & Peter Doyle, *A Model for Optimizing Retail Space Allocations*, 27 MGMT. SCI. 822, 822 (1981) (discussing a space-allocation model relying on product space elasticities, inter-product cross elasticities, different product profit margins, and inventory and handling costs).

label products,[19] the economic incentives facing retailers have shifted. When a supplier owns a popular brand, the supplier is often able to obtain higher margins on the product vis-à-vis the retailer.[20] The retailer may consider the product necessary to attract consumers and hence may have reduced bargaining power in dealing with the supplier. If the retailer owns or controls a private label brand, the retailer may obtain a higher gross margin on the private label because the retailer owns the goodwill of the brand.[21] If the private label is popular and draws customers away from other brands, the retailer also will have more bargaining power in dealing with suppliers of the other brands.[22] Category management, coupled with computer databases, allows a retailer to determine better the competitive and profitability interplay between its own private label products and other products.[23]

Retailing also has become more sophisticated in the display of products. Products with consumer appeal can draw a consumer's attention to an area where a purchase decision will hopefully occur.

---

19.   Robert L. Steiner, *The Nature and Benefits of National Brand/Private Label Competition*, 24 REV. INDUS. ORG. 105, 106 (2004) (citing upward growth for private label food and non-food grocery store products sold in supermarkets, mass merchants, and drug chains in 2000, resulting in a private label market share of 28.1% of unit volume); *Private Label Keeps Nibbling at Food Share-Food and Consumables*, DSN RETAILING TODAY, Sept. 22, 2003, http://findarticles.com/p/articles/mi_m0FNP/_is_18_42/ai_108312341 (citing a 2003 J.P. Morgan study that found that from July 1999 until June 2003, private label in 85 food categories grew 11% while the categories grew 7.8%; private label gained share in 65 categories while name-brand gained in 17).

20.   Steiner, *supra* note 19, at 123.

21.   *See id.* at 108 (summarizing prior studies showing "the tendency for leading advertised brands to have lower [retail gross margins] than lesser known manufacturers' brands and [private labels] is one of the key regularities in consumer goods industries").

22.   *Id.* at 120-22. A manufacturer's and retailer's relative margins depend on how willing consumers are to switch to other products within the store and on how willing consumers are to switch stores if the retail price of their product is too high. *Id.* at 120.

23.   *See* George Baltas & Peter Doyle, *A Flexible Model for Consumer Choice in Packaged Goods Markets*, 40 J. MKT. RES. SOC'Y 141 (1998) (noting that retailer brands have grown in the United Kingdom, forcing new competitors to go for segmentation and positioning); Robert L. Steiner, *Category Management—A Pervasive, New Vertical Format*, 15 ANTITRUST 77, 79 (2001).

Once the consumer's attention has been attracted, the consumer may be induced to purchase complementary products (for example, salsa when tortilla chips are being purchased) or higher profit items such as the retailer's private label.[24] Through category management and the use of computer databases, a retailer can optimize its display strategies.

Retail chains, especially those with significant market share, can be highly sought-after venues for suppliers, just as some products can be highly sought-after items for a retailer to carry.[25] Category management gives retailers a perspective to understand better and to maximize the potential of their own stores, not only in the sale of products to consumers but also in negotiations with suppliers on pricing, promotion, and advertising.

C. Category Captains

The practice of using category captains is an outgrowth of category management.[26] Generally, a category captain is a supplier to whom the retailer delegates (to a greater or lesser extent) responsibility for a particular category.

Retailers commonly appoint a savvy supplier as the "captain" for a particular category and then rely on that supplier for category insights and strategic recommendations that can boost volume and profitability.[27] The usual rationale for appointing one or more category captains for a category is the supplier's specialized and in-depth knowledge of products in the category. The category captain often provides services to the retailer on an unpaid basis.

---

24.   Fiona Scott Morton & Florian Zettelmeyer, *The Strategic Positioning of Store Brands in Retailer–Manufacturer Negotiations*, 24 REV. INDUS. ORG. 161, 162 (2004) (arguing that retailers have an incentive to position store brands as close substitutes to leading national brands).

25.   *See* Toys "R" Us, Inc. v. FTC, 221 F.3d 928, 930 (7th Cir. 2000) (finding that the large retail share held by Toys "R" Us made it a "critical outlet" for toy manufacturers).

26.   *See* NIELSEN MKTG. RESEARCH, *supra* note 1, at 44-45.

27.   *Id.* at 103; *see also* FED. TRADE COMM'N, SLOTTING ALLOWANCES IN THE RETAIL GROCERY INDUSTRY: SELECTED CASE STUDIES IN FIVE PRODUCT CATEGORIES 12 (2003), *available at* http://www.ftc.gov/os/2003/11/slottingallowancerpt031114.pdf ("A category captain typically is a leading supplier's employee, who is responsible for recommending to the retailer an optimal product mix and promotional plans for a particular product category.").

Suppliers historically have made suggestions and comments to retailers about the sale of the supplier's own products, as well as generally about the product category. Category captaincy is an extension of that historical relationship. Duties performed by a category captain can vary widely, including but not limited to (1) merely commenting about present and future products in the category; (2) recommending which products the retailer should carry; or (3) recommending how the retailer should display, price, promote, or advertise products. Category captaincy also can involve the retailer's sharing with the captain otherwise undisclosed information from other suppliers about their pricing and marketing initiatives.[28]

Category captaincy is the main focus of this publication. Sharing responsibility and information with a category captain raises competitive issues that are not as pronounced when a retailer manages the category alone. Although a category captain can provide valuable expertise and assistance to a retailer, the category captain also may act in a self-interested fashion that, if not checked by the retailer, may prejudice the interests of other suppliers of the product, the retailer, or consumers.

D. Various Category Captaincy Structures

Wide variation in the structuring of category captaincy exists, just as a wide range of duties exist that can be given to a category captain. Possible category management structures include those in which (1) the retailer makes its own decisions without the assistance or involvement of a category captain, (2) the retailer appoints one category captain per category, (3) the retailer appoints two or more suppliers as category captains for a category, and (4) the same supplier is appointed separately by two or more retailers to be their category captains. As described in more detail in the following chapters, each structure requires its own antitrust analysis.

---

28.   *See* NIELSEN MKTG. RESEARCH, *supra* note 1, at 165 ("Under these alliances, manufacturers and retailers will share data resources as well as macrocosmic and microcosmic market knowledge and category insights. Each party will strive to advocate the other's strategic objectives and to cooperate in a joint effort to achieve them—so long as the effort produces a 'win-win' result.").

CHAPTER II

ECONOMIC PERSPECTIVES ON CATEGORY MANAGEMENT

This chapter provides an economic overview of category management, with a focus on the use of category captains. It discusses the appropriate measure of competitive performance, assesses the general nature of competition in retail markets, explains both the efficiency-enhancing and possible anticompetitive effects of category captains, and examines how empirical analysis can attempt to identify when a category captain's practices are on balance procompetitive or anticompetitive. This overview provides the necessary economic foundation for the antitrust analysis of category management practices, which is discussed in Chapter III.

A. Category Management vs. Brand Management

As discussed in Chapter I, category management is sometimes compared to the earlier approach of brand management. In both approaches, the retailer's over-arching objectives are the same—namely, to offer products that consumers want to buy, display them in ways that lead consumers to purchase them, and price them at levels that result in maximum profits. A retailer that practices brand management takes a narrower focus with respect to pricing and other competitive decisions than one that practices category management. Given the narrower focus, antitrust concerns are less likely when a retailer makes brand management decisions that by definition are limited to a single upstream supplier.[1] Unlike category management, brand management decisions usually are made without express involvement of an upstream supplier serving as category captain.[2]

---

1. One potential exception to this might arise when an upstream supplier with a significant share of a relevant downstream market uses brand management practices to inhibit or deter entry and expansion by its fringe competitors.

2. For a discussion of the evolution from brand management to category management, see generally Suman Basuroy, Murali K. Mantrala &

13

By contrast, category management involves retailers making decisions (perhaps with recommendations from its category captain) across multiple competing brands, taking into account the interactions among them.

When a retailer moves from brand management to category management, the economic effects bear some resemblance to those that arise when competing branded products merge. Indeed there is a conceptual parallel between category management and the more familiar differentiated products merger analysis.[3] Both category management theory and differentiated products merger analysis predict that an increase in the price of one branded product will induce some consumers to switch to alternative products, whether branded or private label. Profit-maximizing decisions in both contexts will account for the magnitudes of these effects, which are captured by the relevant own-price and cross-price elasticities.

B. Competition in Retail Markets

Because category management is a practice used in retailing, any economic assessment of category management must be grounded in an economic understanding of retailing. Retail markets are, in the main, fiercely competitive.[4] Entry by new retailers and expansion by existing retailers occurs constantly and new retail formats (such as the Internet) have emerged. Consequently, retailer profits tend to be at competitive levels across many segments, ranging from supermarkets to apparel, from gasoline stations to drug stores. For instance, according to the Food and Marketing Institute, grocery store chains' net profits after taxes as a percent of sales have fluctuated between 0.93 percent and 1.84

Rockney G. Walters, *The Impact of Category Management on Retailer Prices and Performance: Theory and Evidence*, 65 J. MKTG. 16 (2001).

3.   *See id.* (using a differentiated products model to assess the impacts from category management). For a discussion of the differentiated products model in the context of merger analysis, see generally Jerry A. Hausman, Gregory Leonard & J. Douglas Zona, *Competitive Analysis with Differentiated Products*, 34 ANNALES D'ECONOMIE ET DE STASTIQUE 159 (1994); Gregory J. Werden & Luke M. Froeb, *The Effects of Mergers in Differentiated Products Industries: Logit Demand and Merger Policy*, 10 J.L. ECON. & ORG. 407 (1994).

4.   See the discussion below on the thin profit margins earned by firms in the retail sector, and the frequency of entry and exit. Low profits and ease of entry and exit are hallmarks of competitive markets.

percent over the decade between 1993 and 2007, with no particular trend upwards or downwards during this period.[5]

C. The Appropriate Measure of Competitive Performance

A retailer selects a company or one of the company's employees as a category captain to help the retailer decide which products to carry, how to display them, and what prices to charge. Because a retailer typically wants someone knowledgeable about the array of products available in the category, category captains typically are suppliers of one or more products in the category at issue. Category captains accordingly are typically in a vertical relationship with the downstream retailer.[6] Vertical relationships can have both efficiency enhancing and competition reducing properties.

Economic theory teaches that in order for a category captain's practices to harm competition and consumers, the category captain or the retailer must possess market power in its market, absent a horizontal conspiracy at either level.[7] If both the supplier/category captain and the retailer operate in competitive markets, a category captain's vertical practices are not likely to threaten competition. This follows from the widely accepted proposition that a vertical restraint generally cannot harm competition when applied in otherwise competitive markets.[8]

The analysis differs, of course, when one or both parties possess market power. When the supplier/category captain has market power, it

---

5.   *See* Food Marketing Institute, Supermarket Facts: Grocery Store Chains Net Profit – Percent of Sales (Dec. 2008), http://www.fmi.org/docs/ facts_figs/Net%20Profit%20Percent%20of%20Sales2008.pdf.

6.   *See, e.g.*, Kenneth Glazer, Brian R. Henry & Jonathan Jacobson, *Antitrust Implications of Category Management: Resolving the Horizontal/ Vertical Characterization Debate*, ANTITRUST SOURCE, July 2004, *available at* http://www.abanet.org/antitrust/at-source/04/07/Jul04-Cat Mgmt7=23.pdf. For a contrary view, see Thomas B. Leary, A Second Look at Category Management (May 17, 2004), http://www.ftc.gov/ speeches/leary/040519categorymgmt.pdf (arguing that aspects of category management are horizontal).

7.   *See, e.g.*, DENNIS W. CARLTON & JEFFREY M. PERLOFF, MODERN INDUSTRIAL ORGANIZATION ch. 16 (4th ed. 2005).

8.   *See, e.g.*, A. Douglas Melamed, Address before the American Bar Association Antitrust Section: Exclusionary Vertical Agreements (April 2, 1998), *available at* http://www.usdoj.gov/atr/public/speeches/1623.pdf ("[T]he theory would suggest that proof of market power should always be required to condemn an exclusionary vertical agreement . . . .").

might be able to use its position as category captain to disadvantage its competitors in ways that harm competition and consumers.[9] Consumers might be harmed if the category captain's practices led to generally higher prices or reduced product quality or output. Of course, if these outcomes reduced the profits of the retailer that chose the supplier to be the category captain, then the retailer may well take steps to reverse or prevent the reduction in its profitability and, in doing so, reverse or prevent the harm to consumers.[10] A retailer could choose another supplier to be category captain, retain greater control over the category's product selection, display, and pricing decisions, or monitor more closely the conduct of the category captain. In such cases, the retailer's pursuit of profits also would tend to enhance consumers' interests.

When the retailer has market power, but upstream suppliers do not, then it seems unlikely that the appointment of a category captain would diminish competition among the upstream suppliers. While the retailer might gain knowledge to increase the retailer's profits further, perhaps by choosing or presenting a selection of products more attractive to consumers, the category captain would likely not be an independent cause of retailer market power. Further, any retailer, including one with market power, prefers that the suppliers of products available to the retailer compete vigorously. Hence, a retailer with market power normally would not have an incentive to implement practices that create

---

9.   It is not sufficient, of course, to rely on a practice's impact on rivals to determine its impact on competition. The practice's impact on consumers is what matters. A manufacturer/category captain could make recommendations to the retailer that harm the category captain's competitors while benefiting the retailer and consumers. For instance, if the category captain develops a new product that a significant number of consumers prefer, the new product's introduction, at the recommendation of the category captain, will improve consumer welfare by increasing the category captain's sales relative to its competitors.

10.   Far thornier issues arise if the category captain's practices increase the profits of both the captain and the retailer, but the retailer's profit could have been higher yet if the captain had made decisions solely in the retailer's best interest instead of ones that also benefited the category captain. One issue is whether the retailer can detect such an outcome, that is, determine that its profits are reduced relative to an alternative outcome. A second issue is whether the retailer can develop any means to deter such behavior by the category captain at the outset even if it can be detected at a later time. Competing suppliers will be highly motivated to inform the retailer about the captain's conduct, but may not know of the captain's internal decisions.

or enhance market power held by its category captain or any of its other upstream suppliers.[11]

1. *Private Label Products*

One complication to this proposition is that retailers have increasingly been introducing private label products, which carry a retailer's name on the label or a brand name exclusive to the retailer. In this way, the retailer is operating at both the upstream supplier level as well as at the downstream retail level and is, in essence, a competitor of its own category captain and the category captain's rivals. According to some reports, private label sales of grocery products in the United States were approximately 16 percent in 2006, with even higher percentages reported in European countries.[12]

Private label products can complicate the analysis of category captains because retailers offering private label products may have a vested interest in protecting the profits generated by those products. The placement and pricing of other branded products may be affected by the retailer's incentive to profit from private label sales. Several economic analyses have examined the retailers' incentives to introduce and position private label products to differentiate themselves vis-à-vis other retailers.[13] One interesting finding from these studies is that retailers

---

11. A possible exception might be where the captain is giving the retailer services or benefits not provided to other retailers, a topic discussed in chapter 6.

12. *See, e.g.*, Alan M. Field, *The Rise of Private Labels*, GULF SHIPPER, February 27, 2006, at 10. *See generally* Fabian Berges-Sennou, Philippe Bontems & Vincent Requillart, *Economics of Private Labels: A Survey of the Literature*, 2 J. AGRIC. & FOOD INDUS. ORG. 1037 (2004).

13. *See, e.g.*, Serdar Sayman, Stephen Hoch & Jagmohan Raju, *Positioning of Store Brands*, 21 MKTG. SCI. 378 (2002) (noting that a retailer may have incentive to target its store brand directly against a leading national brand); Fiona Scott-Morton & Florian Zettelmeyer, *The Strategic Positioning of Store Brands in Retailer–Manufacturer Negotiations*, 24 REV. INDUS. ORG. 161 (2004) (arguing retailers can profit by using private label products to introduce a product as a relatively close substitute to a leading national brand, a strategy that would not be adopted by a rival upstream national brand); Jorge Tarzijan, *Strategic Effects of Private Labels and Horizontal Integration*, 14 INT'L REV. OF RETAIL, DISTRIB. & CONSUMER RES. 321 (2004) (noting that retailers introduce private labels to improve their bargaining position vis-à-vis producers of leading national brands).

may have a unilateral profit incentive to drop secondary national or regional brands and replace them with private label store brands because retailers can earn greater margins on private label brands than on secondary brands. Consequently, the retailer that sells a private label product and the category captain may each benefit from the removal of secondary brands. As a result, a decision to drop a non-leading brand may be due to the downstream retailer's incentives and profits, not to manipulation by the category captain.[14]

2. Local Market Issues

One competitive concern occurs when a number of retailers in a geographic area collectively possess market power. In this situation, the retailers might each choose the same upstream supplier to serve as category captain in the hopes that a common category captain might improve the retailers' understanding of the products carried, as well as the prices charged, by their rivals, thereby facilitating a coordinated price increase in the category.

Local retailers on occasion can possess relatively large shares of the downstream retail markets in which they compete. On a national or regional level, some retailers may be large enough to become particularly important customers for their upstream suppliers, regardless of their share of sales in any particular local market. Wal-Mart, for instance, can be a critically important customer to certain of its upstream suppliers. When a retailer commands a large share of a local market, or controls significant sales across multiple local markets, it might be able to exercise "buyer power" and obtain lower prices or preferential treatment from its suppliers.

D. Efficiencies from Category Management and Category Captains

The primary efficiency attributable to category captains derives from the superior information possessed by the upstream supplier as to consumer preferences for the products in the category, and perhaps for those products complementary to the category as well.[15] When this

---

14. One study found that retailers that introduce private labels tend to disadvantage "second tier" national brands but not "first tier" national brands because the retailer's store brand is a closer substitute for the second tier brands. Koen Pauwels & Shuba Srinivasan, *Who Benefits from Store Brand Entry?*, 23 MKTG. SCI. 364 (2004).

15. One example of complementary products is potato chips and dips.

information is made available to a downstream retailer, the retailer is more likely to make decisions regarding product selection, placement, and pricing that consumers prefer.

At any given time, a retailer can sell tens of thousands of separate items. It is therefore a considerable task to choose which items to carry, how to display them, and how to price them. At the same time, a retailer does not have the economic incentive to track and analyze consumer preferences in each of the categories of products carried in its stores. A retailer's primary goal is to attract the consumer to the store and stimulate a purchase of products within the store—the retailer often cares relatively little whether a consumer chooses brand X or brand Y. Suppliers, by contrast, care very much which brand is chosen and are incentivized to collect and analyze detailed data on consumer preferences within a product category.

Scanner data from multiple retailers track consumer purchases on a product-by-product basis and provide a means for a supplier to track the sales of its own products relative to those of its rivals.[16] A supplier's review of data from multiple retailers can provide a robust basis to predict consumer response to changes in the relative prices, display, and promotion of the category's various products in a retailer's stores. Such information, in addition to being valuable to the supplier, can put the upstream supplier in a position to help downstream retailers make decisions regarding pricing and new product introductions that benefit consumers.[17]

A second benefit of category captaincy is the more efficient utilization of personnel. A category captain can be delegated a variety of tasks by the retailer—e.g., preparation of shelf display diagrams,

---

16.   Other means include surveys of the store's customers and targeted market research using data other than scanner data.

17.   The FTC notes that "the manufacturer may know things like the times of year when a product will sell best, the kinds of promotions that are most effective in moving the product, or the kinds of complementary goods that might be advantageously displayed in adjacent space." FED. TRADE COMM'N, REPORT ON THE FEDERAL TRADE COMMISSION WORKSHOP ON SLOTTING ALLOWANCES AND OTHER MARKETING PRACTICES IN THE GROCERY INDUSTRY 48 (2001) [hereinafter SLOTTING ALLOWANCES WORKSHOP], *available at* http://www.ftc.gov/os/2001/02/slotting allowancesreportfinal.pdf. This argument has also appeared in marketing literature. *See, e.g.*, Rakesh Niraj & Chakravarthi Narasimhan, Vertical Information Sharing in Distribution Channels (July 2004), *available at* http://papers.ssrn.com/ sol3/papers.cfm?abstract_id=903988.

preparation of promotional calendars, oversight of shelf resets or shelf relabeling, policing compliance by local stores and other suppliers with shelf display diagrams and other retailer policies, and reviews of displays and consumer pricing at competitive retailers. The shifting of these tasks from retailer to category captain ordinarily would have no net effect on product cost, as whatever reduction of personnel time was gained by the retailer could be offset by the increase in personnel time borne by the captain. However, to the extent that the captain can use its employees already in the field, the captain may be able accomplish these tasks more efficiently than the retailer.

A third possible procompetitive benefit is the alleviation of the category captain's concerns about free-riding. Supplier payments for promotional opportunities and retail shelf space are a common phenomenon in retail distribution. Suppliers are willing to offer payments to a retailer to stock products, to promote or advertise their products, and to allow placement on shelves, special displays, and end of aisle locations.

Shelf space payments (payments by suppliers to retailers for premier retail locations such as the end of aisles or eye level shelf space) have become increasingly important in the supermarket industry,[18] as well as other retail sectors such as drug stores, and bookstores.[19] Marketing studies have demonstrated that suppliers can increase sales by using promotional expenditures to purchase valuable shelf space.[20] Promotional shelf space is therefore important to suppliers, especially when the supplier supplies differentiated products and uses promotional

18.   *See* FED. TRADE COMM'N, SLOTTING ALLOWANCES IN THE RETAIL GROCERY INDUSTRY: SELECTED CASE STUDIES IN FIVE PRODUCT CATEGORIES (2003), *available at* http://www.ftc.gov/os/2003/11/slotting allowancerpt031114.pdf; SLOTTING ALLOWANCES WORKSHOP, *supra* note 17.

19.   *See* Iris Rosenthal, *Slotting Fees Continue to Spark Controversy in Retailing*, 135 DRUG TOPICS 81 (1991); James Surowiecki, *Paying to Play*, NEW YORKER, July 12, 2004, at 42; Jeffrey A. Trachtenberg, *Is Selling Books Like Selling Frozen Food?*, WALL ST. J., May 20, 2002, at B1.

20.   *See* Charles Areni et al., *Point-of-Purchase Displays, Product Organization, and Brand Purchase Likelihoods*, 27 J. ACAD. MKTG. SCI. 248 (1999); Xavier Dreze et al., *Shelf Management and Space Elasticity*, 70 J. RETAILING 301 (1994); Adam Rennhoff, Paying for Shelf Space: An Investigation of Merchandising Allowances in the Grocery Industry (Food Marketing Policy Center, Research Report No. 84, Oct. 2004), *available at* http://www.fmpc.uconn.edu/publications/rr/rr84.pdf.

expenditures to increase sales instead of reducing its wholesale price. A retailer, however, does not necessarily benefit when a consumer shifts from one brand to another in the retailer's store; the retailer likely would have made money either way.[21] A supplier uses shelf space payments to align the interests of retailers with its own interest in promotional shelf space; both gain incremental revenue from the supplier's use of the shelf space for the promotion.[22] The same dynamic exists for a supplier's participation in a retailer's advertisements and in-store promotions. Certain forms of promotional and shelf space exclusivity can address the concern that the retailer might have incentives that differ from the supplier making the promotional payment.

The sales increase generated by a promotion, advertisement, or promotional shelf space can be undercut if the retailer is involved in other promotional activity in the category at the same time or does not execute the promotion effectively. In particular, when decisions regarding promotion, pricing, and product placement reside with the retailer or with a rival supplier serving as category captain, these parties' incentives to maximize their own profits could allow them to undercut the promotional expenditures made by the original supplier, thereby diluting the value of this investment to the original supplier. By assuming the role of category captain, the supplier has additional assurance that its payments to the retailer effectively promote the sale of its products and that its programs will not be undercut.[23]

---

21. A retailer gains an additional benefit if the customer is induced to purchase a product he or she normally would not have bought, or if the promotion attracts customers who otherwise would have gone to a competing retailer, or if the promoted product carries a higher retail margin.

22. Benjamin Klein & Joshua D. Wright, *The Economics of Slotting Contracts*, 50 J.L. & ECON. 421 (2007). Klein and Murphy originally articulated the problem of insufficient retailer supply of promotion. *See* Benjamin Klein & Kevin M. Murphy, *Vertical Restraints as Contract Enforcement Mechanisms*, 31 J.L. & ECON. 265 (1988).

23. The category captain arrangement can lead to the equivalent of a de facto limited or full exclusive contract if the captain has the responsibility for allocating shelf space or promotions, does so to the exclusion of other competitors, and is not constrained by the retailer. *See* Joshua D. Wright, Antitrust Analysis of Category Management: *Conwood Co. v. United States Tobacco Co.* (George Mason Univ. Law and Econ. Research Paper No. 06-38, 2006), *available at* http://ssrn com/abstract_id=945178.

To the extent a category captain or any other supplier faces less risk of uncertainty as to its promotions, promotional payments to retailers will tend to increase, and hence tend to lower the cost of the product to the consumer. Whether that sequence of events inures to the benefit of the consumer depends, to some degree, on whether the category captain arrangement leads to any of the anticompetitive outcomes described below.

E. Competitive Concerns with Category Captains

The competitive concerns associated with category captains include: (1) foreclosure of potential rival suppliers from access to retailers and consumers, or diminishing the quality of their access (e.g., by providing rivals with less preferred shelf position, or introducing fewer new products produced by rivals); (2) collusion among competing retailers orchestrated through a category captain in a "hub-and-spoke" arrangement, thereby reducing competition at the retail level and raising prices to consumers; and (3) coordination among upstream suppliers facilitated by the category captain's observations of the rivals' activities in multiple retailers in a geographic market, thereby reducing competition at the supplier level and elevating prices to consumers.

In general, determining whether a category captain arrangement will produce any of these competitive concerns requires a careful assessment of the incentives and options facing all of the parties—upstream suppliers, downstream retailers, and consumers. Each of these parties might be able to take actions, either unilaterally or in conjunction with retailers or other upstream rivals, to defeat or deter any attempt by the category captain to raise prices or reduce output. Each of these competitive concerns is described below, with discussion of empirical analyses that might discern anticompetitive outcomes.

1. Foreclosure of Upstream Rivals

Most economic analyses of category captains focus on the possibility that the category captain will have the incentive and ability to reduce competition by favoring its own products relative to those of its branded and unbranded rivals.[24] The basic concern is straightforward and

---

24.   *See generally* Basuroy et al., *supra* note 2; Leary, A Second Look at Category Management, *supra* note 6. Concerns for anticompetitive self-dealing arise frequently in industries where firms are vertically integrated, and economists have attempted to discern whether vertically integrated

articulated clearly in a 2001 FTC Staff Report: "A captain that is able to control decisions about product placement and promotions could hinder the entry or expansion of other suppliers, leading to less variety and possibly higher prices."[25]

A category captain potentially could deprive its rivals of the opportunity to compete for distribution on the merits. Exclusive distribution arrangements may produce anticompetitive effects if a dominant supplier can control a sufficient amount of distribution for a sufficient period of time, such that rivals are effectively prevented from reaching minimum efficient scale.[26] However, if a retailer has a relatively small share of retail sales of the products in the category in the relevant geographic area, the retailer's installation of a category captain likely would not have a significant harmful effect on competition and on consumers.[27]

One of the greatest difficulties in assessing the effects of category captain-suggested changes is determining whether those changes benefit consumers. A retailer's removal or reduction of products of inferior quality or lesser consumer appeal is economically rational, whether or

---

firms have the incentive and ability to distort competition in ways that harm consumers. For studies that examine the effects from laws that prohibit gasoline refiners from vertically integrating into the operation of retail service stations, see generally Asher A. Blass & Dennis W. Carlton, *The Choice of Organizational Form in Gasoline Retailing and the Costs of Laws Limiting that Choice*, 44 J.L. & ECON. 511 (2001), and Michael G. Vita, *Regulatory Restrictions on Vertical Integration and Control: The Competitive Impact of Gasoline Divorcement Policies*, 18 J. REG. ECON. 217 (2000).

25. SLOTTING ALLOWANCES WORKSHOP, *supra* note 17, at 50-51. This FTC staff report also raised the concern that the category captain could obtain sensitive competitive information from its rivals and use that information to distort competition; we subsume this concern into the foreclosure concern described in this chapter.

26. *See* Benjamin Klein, *Exclusive Dealing as Competition for Distribution 'On the Merits'*, 12 GEO. MASON L. REV. 119, 122–25 (2004) (discussing necessary conditions for such a strategy to result in anticompetitive effects).

27. Indeed, it is commonly accepted that retailers without market power who act as exclusive dealers for a particular manufacturer generate benefits to consumers as the exclusive dealing arrangement serves to align the incentives of the manufacturer and the retailer. *See generally* CARLTON & PERLOFF, *supra* note 7, at ch. 12 (discussing vertical restraints); Howard P. Marvel, *Exclusive Dealing*, 25 J.L. & ECON. 1 (1982).

not a category captain recommended the change. Moreover, it can be economically rational to reduce a retailer's costs by limiting the number of suppliers to be managed and coordinated. Consumers, however, may not favor the reduction in varieties available at the retailer's stores. Assessing future consumer demand and balancing it against cost efficiencies is a daunting task involving predictive uncertainty and trial-and-error. Consumer response to changes in product selection, display, promotion, and pricing may not be immediate and may require consumer observation over a period of time to determine success or failure.

Additionally, measuring the impact of category management decisions is difficult. Empirical testing of these decisions is relatively rare in the economic literature and can lead to different conclusions.[28] In principle, retail scanner data could be used.[29] Retailers and suppliers, especially if sophisticated, commonly do temporal analyses in the same store or set of stores. These before-and-after reviews can be useful but are quite limited as a basis for market-wide inferences.

---

28. *Compare* Basuroy et al., *supra* note 2 (demonstrating that the introduction of category management, rather than brand management, in the laundry detergent segment at a single retailer was associated with higher average retail prices, reduced wholesale prices, lower sales, and higher retailer category profits), *with* Klein & Wright, *supra* note 22 (demonstrating that slotting contracts and retail competitive conditions are inconsistent with anticompetitive theories using aggregate margin data), *and* Joshua D. Wright, *Slotting Contracts and Consumer Welfare*, 74 ANTITRUST L.J. 439 (2007) (examining consumer welfare metrics such as price, output and product variety to conclude that slotting arrangements do not harm consumers), *and* Peter Bronsteen, Kenneth G. Elzinga & David E. Mills, *Price Competition and Slotting Allowances*, 50 ANTITRUST BULL. 267 (2005) (analysis using scanner data to assess the relationship between slotting allowances and the retail prices of cigarettes).

29. For a recent analysis that used scanner data to assess the relationship between slotting allowances and the retail prices of cigarettes, see Bronsteen et al., *supra* note 28. Scanner data aggregate information from individual consumer transactions, and have been used regularly to assess the potential competitive effects from transactions involving branded consumer products. *See e.g.*, Steven Tenn, Estimating Promotional Effects with Retail-Level Scanner Data (Fed. Trade Comm'n Bureau of Economics, Working Paper No. 264, 2006), *available at* http://www.ftc.gov/be/workpapers/wp264.pdf.

2. *Coordination among Competing Retailers*

A second potential competitive concern raised by the practice of category captains is that a single supplier, acting as the category captain for a number of retailers, could serve as the "hub" in a hub-and-spoke conspiracy among the participating retailers. This theory bears some resemblance to the one articulated by the FTC in the *Toys "R" Us* case in which Toys "R" Us was found to have orchestrated an agreement among various toy suppliers not to distribute certain toys through retail outlets other than Toys "R" Us.[30] Similarly, if the category captain has direct influence over product pricing and selection decisions for a significant proportion of retail outlets, the retailers could conceivably coordinate through the category captain to raise retail prices and earn higher margins with the assurance that the other coordinating retailers would abide by the arrangement.

There are a number of factors that could make a hub-and-spoke conspiracy difficult. First, retail distribution is often fluid and differentiated, with few barriers to entry. Consequently, as a practical matter, a vertically managed retailer conspiracy could be difficult to achieve and sustain. The often large number of local retailers could make a conspiracy difficult to form. Mail order and Internet vendors, as well as fringe and new-entrant retailers, could tend to make any such conspiracy unwieldy and difficult to maintain. Additionally, excluded suppliers could tend to disrupt any conspiracy by their constant and aggressive sales efforts, including price promotions. The presence or availability of private label products, as well as the availability of other products to consumers, could create divisive incentives among the conspirators and would tend to decrease the benefit of the conspiracy. The inherent price elasticity of the product that is the subject of the retail price coordination arrangement also could affect the success of the conspiracy; if the product was not essential, the product would likely be more susceptible to consumers diverting or reducing their purchases.

Second, the public nature of retail prices calls into question why a category captain would be helpful in such a conspiracy. Review of competitors' advertisements and visits to their stores can provide a significant amount of market information. There would likely need to be some significant, additional benefit in having a category captain participate in such a conspiracy. There also would need to be some benefit to the category captain to join the conspiracy, presumably in

---

30.   *See* Toys "R" Us, Inc. v. FTC, 221 F.3d 928, 931-32 (7th Cir. 2000).

receiving an increased wholesale price or exclusivity. Rewarding the category captain in this way, however, would reduce the anticompetitive gains the retailers could retain for themselves.

Still, the hub-and-spoke theory may be worth testing empirically with brand-specific sales data (e.g., scanner data) combined with information that identifies the firms chosen to be category captains in various geographic regions and the retailers that chose them.[31] The hypothesis to be tested would be whether retail prices in a particular category are higher in regions where the retailers choose the same category captain.[32] The data requirements for such a project are clearly considerable, as information on the category captains chosen by particular retailers is not readily available.[33]

3. *Coordination among Competing Upstream Suppliers*

The third potential competitive concern raised by the practice of category captains is that rival suppliers could use their role as category captains to facilitate coordination at the upstream (as opposed to the retail) level. This theory posits that when one or more upstream firms are category captains for different retailers in the same geographic market, they are better able to observe other suppliers' actions, which in

---

31. This theory, unlike the foreclosure theory described first, does not require that the category captain possess a significant share of sales in the category. Of course, if the captain has a relatively small share, one would have to explain why the captain would have an economic incentive to facilitate an anticompetitive arrangement that largely benefits the coordinating retailers without improving the captain's small market position.

32. There is some empirical evidence showing that retail prices of first tier national brands tend to rise when a retailer begins offering a private label product in the category. By contrast, prices of second tier national brands, which compete more closely with the store brand, tend to decline following the introduction of private label products. *See* Pauwels & Srinivasan, *supra* note 14.

33. There are a number of factors that could complicate further the analysis. For instance, some of the retailers in the area might set prices across a broader geographic region than others, i.e., have larger geographic "price zones." This implies that the benefits from coordination within a particular area may differ across retailers, which reduces the likelihood of their reaching an agreement in the first place, and reduces the likelihood that the coordinating retailers will abide by the agreement when circumstances change.

turn could facilitate an agreement to raise wholesale prices by improving detection and punishment of possible defections from the agreement. The agreement could be limited to raising wholesale prices; or, it could also encompass not introducing as many new products at the relevant retailers, which would reduce the chances that the agreement would be disrupted by unpredictable consumer reactions to new products.

One might reasonably wonder why a set of upstream suppliers would need to rely on their roles as category captains to establish and maintain a coordinated agreement to raise wholesale prices or diminish the rate of new product introductions. There are two reasons why. First, an agreement to elevate wholesale prices can be difficult to monitor. If a retailer shares with a category captain the wholesale prices being charged by other suppliers, monitoring arguably will be made easier, and a cheating conspirator may thus be detected more quickly. However, where a retailer sets its retail prices by using a uniform mark-up from wholesale price, wholesale price information can be inferred by anyone visiting a store and thus category captaincy may be unnecessary to facilitate such a conspiracy. Second, if the category captains have influence over the retailers' retail prices, an agreement that effectively stabilizes retail prices could eliminate an upstream firm's incentive to "cheat" on the agreement in the first place, an attempt to increase sales by lowering wholesale prices to a retailer would tend to be frustrated if the cheater's retail prices did not decline as well.

These theories can be difficult to test, given the many factors affecting retail distribution. Still, one could in principle test the theories empirically by tracking wholesale and retail prices and new product introductions in markets where several significant firms fulfill the role of category captain as compared with markets where category captains either do not exist or where only one firm tends to provide the bulk of the category captain services to the major retailers.[34] One would then need to control for factors such as differences in consumer demographics and in local retailer concentration and other possible aspects of competitive performance. One also would need to try to account for whatever product selection, pricing, and display decisions were made independently by retailers.

---

34.   Note that in the latter case the "control group" is one where the exercise of unilateral market power by the category captain might be occurring.

F. Conclusion

As a general matter, category captain relationships should be analyzed as vertical restraints. Like most distribution arrangements between suppliers and retailers, category management may generate significant welfare gains for consumers and may produce competitive concerns under only certain conditions. Determining the balance between welfare gains and competitive concerns is complex and fact-intensive, characteristics that suggest the appropriateness of using the rule of reason analysis in the absence of a horizontal conspiracy among retailers or among suppliers. Economic analysis will be challenged, however, by the data complexities of retailing, which may make more difficult the legal counselor's job of assessing antitrust risk under a rule of reason analysis.

CHAPTER III

ANTITRUST ANALYSIS OF CATEGORY MANAGEMENT PRACTICES

As discussed in chapter II, category management has the potential to promote competition, but abuses of the process also may restrain competition by either facilitating collusion among competitors or excluding rivals. This chapter examines the antitrust analysis of category management practices given those two potential effects.

The chapter first addresses the various theories as to how category management might reduce competition among firms competing either at the supplier level or the retailer level. Section 1 of the Sherman Act prohibits any "contract, combination or conspiracy" "in restraint of trade."[1] Section 1 thus prohibits agreements that lead to or facilitate concerted action among competitors that "unreasonably" restrains trade.[2] Category management practices that facilitate collusion may thus violate Section 1.

Category management also has the potential to limit competition by excluding rivals, particularly those of the category captain. Agreements that exclude rivals may unreasonably restrain competition and therefore violate Section 1 of the Sherman Act.[3] In addition, unilateral but exclusionary conduct by a firm with monopoly power may violate Section 2 of the Sherman Act.[4] A determination of liability under either statute in the context of category management practices will generally require an examination of the nature of the agreement or conduct, market power, and any procompetitive justifications for the agreement or conduct.[5]

---

1.   15 U.S.C. § 1.
2.   *See, e.g.*, Monsanto Co. v. Spray-Rite Service Corp., 465 U.S. 752, 768 (1984). For a comprehensive discussion of Section 1, see ABA SECTION OF ANTITRUST LAW, ANTITRUST LAW DEVELOPMENTS 1-224 (6th ed. 2007) ["ALD VI"].
3.   *See generally* ALD VI 1-224.
4.   *See generally id.* at 225-323.
5.   *See generally id.* at 46-77, 225-244.

The chapter begins with a discussion of the FTC's examination of related retail practices.

A. The FTC's View of Related Retail Practices

Historically, the FTC has shown interest in preventing anticompetitive or exclusionary retail practices. In response to Congressional inquiries and a petition for action with regard to slotting allowances,[6] the FTC looked at various category management practices, but declined in reports issued in 2002 and 2003 to condemn the main target of its focus, slotting allowances.[7] The ambivalent findings outlined in the FTC reports are instructive as to why it is difficult to counsel clients on the risk profile of various practices.

None of the practices the FTC examined (slotting allowances, pay-to-stay fees, payments to limit the shelf-space available to a rival, discriminatory payment of access fees) were considered anticompetitive by themselves. The FTC Report questioned whether these practices actually could exclude rivals, and whether any anticompetitive effects outweighed the efficiencies the practices stimulated.[8] The totality of the facts surrounding the suppliers, customers, and markets would determine whether, in a given situation, a specific practice was unreasonable. Commission staff was not really concerned about slotting allowances when they were used to advance the fundamentally procompetitive goal of introducing new products.[9] The report found that in that role slotting allowances served to mitigate some of the risks undertaken by the retailer

---

6. The FTC announced on June 21, 2002, that it would not issue guidelines on the payment of slotting allowances, denying a petition, filed on April 14, 2000, by the Independent Bakers Association, the Tortilla Industry Association, and the National Association of Chewing Gum Manufacturers. Acknowledging the complexity of the situation, the FTC said it would research the matter further. *See* Letter from Donald S. Clark, FTC Secretary, to Robert A. Skitol and Kathleen S. O'Neill (June 19, 2002), *available at* http://www.ftc.gov/os/2002/06/slottingletter.pdf (denying request for guidelines).
7. FED. TRADE COMM'N, REPORT ON THE FEDERAL TRADE COMMISSION WORKSHOP ON SLOTTING ALLOWANCES AND OTHER MARKETING PRACTICES IN THE GROCERY INDUSTRY 48 (2001) [hereinafter SLOTTING ALLOWANCES WORKSHOP], *available at* http://www.ftc.gov/os/2001/02/slottingallowancesreportfinal.pdf.
8. *See id.* at 35-44.
9. *See id.* at 1.

in carrying an untested item.[10] Commission staff noted questions about whether the use of category management and category captains raised a greater risk of collusion and exclusion.[11] The report noted a concern that a category captain might obtain proprietary information about its rivals' marketing plans that would enable it to design a promotional program that would blunt the rivals' marketing efforts.[12] The report, however, did not recommend any specific enforcement activity.

The Commission issued a second report on slotting allowances in November 2003, but it did not conclude that the practices were anticompetitive.[13] The report noted that slotting allowances could be used as a facilitating practice to raise prices, or could be used by a dominant supplier to exclude competition. On the other hand, the report pointed out that slotting allowances could enhance efficiency by ensuring the success of a new product, contributing to the efficient allocation of shelf space, or encouraging suppliers to make investments to stimulate demand.[14] Slotting allowances appeared to be just one type of allowance received by retailers as part of a package of allowances.

The FTC enforcement action most closely related to category management practices came in the FTC action against spice maker McCormick & Company,[15] based on Robinson-Patman Act liability.[16] McCormick was the largest manufacturer of spice and seasoning

---

10. *See id.* at 12–13.

11. *See id.* at 52–54.

12. *See id.* at 50.

13. FED. TRADE COMM'N, SLOTTING ALLOWANCES IN THE RETAIL GROCERY INDUSTRY: SELECTED CASE STUDIES IN FIVE PRODUCT CATEGORIES (2003), *available at* http://www.ftc.gov/os/2003/11/slotting allowancerpt031114.pdf.

14. *Id.; see also* K. Sudhir & Vithala Rao, Are Slotting Allowances Efficiency-Enhancing or Anti-Competitive? (Oct. 26, 2004) (unpublished manuscript, on file with Yale Law School), *available at* http://www.mba.yale.edu/faculty/pdf/slottingallowances.pdf. The study concludes, based on a very limited study, that slotting allowances (1) serve to efficiently allocate scarce retail shelf space, (2) help balance the risk of new product failure between manufacturers and retailers, (3) help manufacturers signal private information about potential success of new product, and (4) serve to widen retail distribution for manufacturers by mitigating retail competition. The authors found little support for anticompetitive rationales.

15. A history of the FTC action against McCormick can be found on the FTC's website, at http://www.ftc.gov/opa/2000/03/mccormick.shtm.

16. 15 U.S.C. § 13.

products, and had only one national competitor for sales of spices to supermarkets. McCormick allegedly violated the Robinson-Patman Act by setting different prices and promotional rates, including the use of payments to guarantee up to 90 percent of the available shelf space. The Commission released a statement that McCormick had not documented a meeting competition defense, and that the disfavored customers had few, if any, alternative sources to purchase spices at the same prices. A key factor in the FTC's decision to bring the action seems to have been the combination of McCormick's dominant market share and its imposition of requirements of near exclusivity upon many of its customers.[17]

The Commission has expressed an interest in how monopsony power and slotting allowances should be considered when evaluating mergers in the retail grocery industry, and, at the same time, it also has recognized that slotting allowances may manifest competition. In a challenge to the Heinz–Beech Nut baby food merger,[18] the FTC noted that one way in which the merger could reduce competition would be in the reduction of competition to get on the shelf (which was reflected in the payment of slotting allowances).

The FTC did raise concerns about specifically regarding category management practices in its review of the acquisition of Gillette by Procter & Gamble.[19] The FTC considered whether the combined category management roles of Gillette and Procter & Gamble were significant enough to increase any anticompetitive effects of the merger of the companies. The FTC concluded that most retailers did not look at broad categories of products (like oral care), and instead focused on individual products, and found that the postmerger entity would not have

---

17. The Commission split 3–2 in the *McCormick* case, with the dissent pointing out that there was no evidence of below-cost sales injuring other suppliers and no evidence that competition among retailers had been injured. *See* McCormick & Co., File No. 961-0050 (dissenting statement of Commissioners Swindle and Leary), *available at* http://www.ftc.gov/os/2000/03/mccormickswindle learysta.htm. The Commission has not brought any subsequent cases attacking discriminatory shelf allowances.

18. *See* FTC v. H.J. Heinz Co., 246 F.3d 708 (D.C. Cir. 2001).

19. *See* Fed. Trade Comm'n, Analysis of Agreement Containing Consent Orders to Aid Public Comment, In the Matter of the Procter & Gamble Company and the Gillette Company, File No. 051-0115 (Sept. 30, 2005), *available at* http://www.ftc.gov/os/caselist/0510115/050930agree 0510115.pdf.

an increased ability to take advantage of its role as category captain for a number of different categories in a store.[20]

B. The Antitrust Analysis of Category Management Practices that May Facilitate Collusion

1. *Category Management with Multiple Category Captains*

A retailer seeking to maximize the amount of marketing input it receives may ask two or more suppliers to act as co-captains of a category, or to have one supplier validate the recommendations of another. By themselves, these practices do not necessarily violate the antitrust laws, but antitrust issues may arise if there is direct interaction between the co-captains.

For example, one potentially problematic scenario is when two captains of a category get together and decide that only their products should appear on the shelves at the retailer. If the retailer ceded authority to the two captains to run the category, there could be antitrust risk. A question would exist as to how the retailer's consent to the situation affects the antitrust analysis.[21]

The appointment of co-captains also raises a risk of information sharing among competitors that might inevitably lead to outright collusion or at least tacit coordination of their competitive activities in selling to retailers. A seller normally would not want to share valuable information with a rival.

2. *The "Hub-and-Spoke" Theory: Knowing Collusion by Retailers*

In a "hub-and-spoke" conspiracy, one party (in this case, the captain) acts as a central point to facilitate a common understanding or agreement among retailers. All of the members of the alleged conspiracy must have some knowledge of the unlawful nature of the project, and there must be a showing that each alleged member knowingly participated.[22]

---

20. *Id.*
21. A category manager providing inaccurate information may be a factor in a court finding antitrust liability. *Cf.* Conwood Co. v. U.S. Tobacco Co., 290 F.3d 768, 776 (6th Cir. 2002).
22. *See* Toys "R" Us, Inc. v. FTC, 221 F.3d 928, 934-35 (7th Cir. 2000); Elder-Beerman Stores Corp. v. Federated Dep't Stores, 459 F.2d 138, 146-47 (6th Cir. 1972); *see also* Kotteakos v. United States, 328 U.S. 750 (1946); *In re* Lupron Mktg. & Sales Practices Litig., 295 F. Supp. 2d 148,

A supplier that acts as a category captain for several retailers will normally obtain information about each retailer's pricing and marketing plans. It would have the ability to act as a central point to facilitate the interchange of this information to enable the retailers to coordinate their marketing activities and reduce competition between them. This kind of risk on the supplier's side would at least be partially addressed by strict confidentiality rules, where employees would be prohibited from sharing information on what competing retailers were doing. In addition to strictly enforced confidentiality rules, a supplier could limit its antitrust exposure by using separate teams of employees to call on different customers, and prohibiting the teams from sharing account information with one another. On the retailer side, a retailer might well choose not to appoint as category captain a supplier that is currently serving in the same role for a competitor.

3. The "Common Price Setter" Theory: Category Captain Sets Prices for Competing Retailers

Can a category captain encounter antitrust liability by "setting" retail prices through its category management activities at competing retailers? Courts have held that where competitors appoint a common sales agent with power to set prices, liability can arise under Section 1.[23] The principle underlying those decisions is that the appointment of a common agent can have the same price fixing effect as a direct horizontal agreement between the competitors.[24] The existence of this line of authority is further reason for the retailer to avoid giving the category

---

165 (D. Mass. 2003); Masco Contractor Servs. E. v. Beals, 279 F. Supp. 2d 699, 708–09 (E.D. Va. 2003); Harlem River Consumers Coop. v. Assoc. Grocers of Harlem, Inc., 408 F. Supp. 1251, 1279 (S.D.N.Y. 1976); Thomas B. Leary, A Second Look at Category Management (May 17, 2004), http://www.ftc.gov/ speeches/leary/040519categorymgmt.pdf.

23.   Citizen Publ'g Co. v. United States, 394 U.S. 131, 134–36 (1969); Va. Excelsior Mills v. FTC, 256 F.2d 538, 540 (4th Cir. 1958).

24.   *See Va. Excelsior Mills*, 256 F.2d at 539-40 (finding a per se violation of Section 1 where competing producers vested pricing power in a single corporate agent). However, joint sales arrangements also can be judged under the rule of reason and be found to be legal where the arrangement is nonexclusive or based on procompetitive justifications. *See* Int'l Healthcare Mgmt. v. Hawaii Coal. for Health, 332 F.3d 600 (9th Cir. 2003).

captain price-setting authority and for the parties to use internal firewalls to safeguard the confidentiality of each retailer's decisions.

4. Conclusions Regarding Collusion Concerns

New methods of marketing and distribution are often embraced enthusiastically by businesspeople. But the role of the antitrust counselor—as part of an overall compliance program—is to make sure that each new practice is evaluated as to the antitrust risk it poses. How would the practice be viewed by customers, competitors, or government enforcers?[25] Most category management activities involve at least an initial agreement: the category manager and retailer will agree on what services will be provided, and what, if any, payments will be made.[26] Spelling out each party's responsibilities clearly, and stating the justifications for or potential benefits from such an arrangement can be the first steps of showing what the parties have and have not agreed to and the reasonableness of the arrangement. This agreement can and should define the expectations of the parties as to how the information will be shared, and make clear that the recommendations that come from the category captain are recommendations, and nothing more, thus preserving the retailer's unilateral decision-making authority.

Retailers often appoint category captains as a way to lower costs (i.e., having a supplier perform tasks and incur costs that would otherwise be borne by the retailer),[27] which, in theory, allows the retailer to pass along lower costs to consumers. While the supplier provides data and suggestions, often the retailer has a market positioning and

---

25. Darren Bush & Betsy Gelb, *When Marketing Practices Raise Antitrust Concerns*, 46 MIT SLOAN MGMT. REV. 73 (2005).

26. Slotting fee payments may tend to be larger from smaller manufacturers where the retailer perceives a need for compensation for risk taking. Larger manufacturers, with a more established reputation, and who are able to provide more comprehensive marketing data together with their products, tend to pay lower slotting fees. Akshay Rao & Humaira Mahi, *The Price of Launching a New Product: Empirical Evidence on Factors Affecting the Relative Magnitude of Slotting Allowances*, 22 MKTG. SCI. 246 (2002).

27. Sarah Ellison, *Retailers' Appetite for Top Sellers Has Food Firms Slimming Down*, WALL ST. J., Oct. 28, 2004, at A1.

competitive strategy already decided, and it is merely up to the supplier to provide information consistent with that strategy.[28]

The category management process may facilitate more efficient responses to consumer needs, yielding higher profits for sellers and greater satisfaction for buyers, yet like every system of enhanced communication among customers and competitors, the boundary between procompetitive and anticompetitive conduct can be unclear. The following points may be important in advising clients.

- Although much Section 1 litigation revolves around attempts to disprove the existence of an unlawful agreement, where category management is concerned, a written agreement may be an important element of antitrust risk management. The agreement could make clear that the supplier is providing suggestions only, and that the retailer will retain decision-making authority for product assortment, shelf-positioning, prices, promotions, etc.

- All aspects of a category management program should have a business justification. If there is no easily understood procompetitive reason why a certain practice is employed, the antitrust risk of that practice increases.

- The category captain should behave responsibly, and if it is willing to accept the role of captain, it should recommend what it objectively thinks is best for the category.

- The written agreement should contain confidentiality provisions to ensure that the supplier is prohibited from sharing a retailer's marketing information with the retailer's competitors.

- The category captain should limit the sharing of information internally so that information from competing retailers is not used or distributed inappropriately.

- There is less antitrust (and other) risk if employees are trained in the precise parameters of what they can and cannot do. A compliance program can ensure that the boundaries of proper activities are not crossed.

- While a retailer may want two or more suppliers to serve as co-captains, the horizontal communications between the category captains can increase antitrust risk. Therefore, if the customer chooses this arrangement, then "rules of engagement" should be followed that control what information is shared between the

---

28.   Venkatesh Shankar & Ruth Bolton, *An Empirical Analysis of Determinants of Retailer Pricing Strategy*, 23 MKTG. SCI. 28 (2004).

competitors and prohibit any anticompetitive agreements. The more knowledge and involvement the retailer has in the horizontal dealings between the co-captains, generally the less risk there should be.

- It is prudent to limit communications, direct or indirect, through a common category captain as to confidential and competitively-significant subjects.
- A category captain should avoid allowing one retailer to affect the captain's category management decisions for another retailer.

C. The Antitrust Analysis of Category Management Practices that May Exclude Rivals

1. *Exclusive Dealing*

Exclusive dealing is perhaps the most obvious area of concern for the category captaincy relationship.[29] Exclusive dealing has been described as a form of monopolization that occurs through "raising [one's] rivals' distribution costs by eliminating their access to downstream markets."[30] A large market position, together with the power to determine retailers' plans for stocking shelves and ordering from competing suppliers, may grant the captain the power to exclude its competitors' products.[31]

The analysis of exclusive dealing focuses on the degree of impact the exclusive dealing has on the market in question.[32] To make out an

---

29. *See* Tampa Elec. Co. v. Nashville Co., 365 U.S. 320, 321–22 (1961) (reversing lower court holding that a requirements contract was illegal under Section 3 of the Clayton Act); Standard Oil Co. v. United States, 337 U.S. 293, 314 (1949) (Section 3 of the Clayton Act); Lepage's Inc. v. 3M, 324 F.3d 141, 145 (3d Cir. 2003) (reviewing claims under Section 2 of the Sherman Act on appeal from jury verdict holding defendant liable for violating Section 2 and not liable for violating Section 1 of the Sherman Act or Section 3 of the Clayton Act); United States v. Microsoft Corp., 253 F.3d 34, 84 (D.C. Cir. 2001) (Section 1 of the Sherman Act). *See generally* ABA SECTION OF ANTITRUST LAW, ANTITRUST LAW DEVELOPMENTS 210–21 (6th ed. 2007).

30. NicSand, Inc. v. 3M Co., 457 F.3d 534, 543 (6th Cir. 2006), *vacated and superceded*, 507 F.3d 442 (6th Cir. 2007) (en banc).

31. *See LePage's*, 324 F.3d at 163.

32. *See* Jefferson Parish Hosp. Dist. No. 2 v. Hyde, 466 U.S. 2, 45 (1984) (concurring opinion) ("Exclusive dealing is an unreasonable restraint on trade only when a significant fraction of buyers or sellers are frozen out of a market by the exclusive deal."); *Tampa Elec. Co.*, 365 U.S. at 332–

exclusive dealing claim, a plaintiff must show the requisite exclusive agreement, sufficient market power to demonstrate that the challenged agreement threatens reduced output or higher prices, and market foreclosure sufficient for injury to competition.[33] Sufficient market foreclosure is properly understood as a question of both the degree of foreclosure and the duration of the foreclosure.[34] If the plaintiff makes a prima facie case for exclusive dealing, the defendant may counter with compelling defenses, which are those that "relate[] directly or indirectly to the enhancement of consumer welfare," such as efficiencies gained by the conduct.[35] Then a court will consider less restrictive alternatives, and sometimes engage in balancing.[36]

As with other conduct, the reality of a category captain's ability to exclude its competitors is subject to a host of factors. A large retailer—like Kroger Co., whose executive testified in *Conwood* that a category captain would be "committing suicide" to attempt to use its position to

---

34 (foreclosure of less than 1% of market through requirements contract insufficient to state claim of exclusive dealing under Section 3 of the Clayton Act).

33.   *LePage's*, 324 F.3d at 157–58. *See generally* 11 HERBERT HOVENKAMP, ANTITRUST LAW ¶ 1821, at 167 (2d ed. 2005); Edward A. Snyder & Thomas E. Kauper, *Misuses of the Antitrust Laws: The Competitor Plaintiff*, 90 MICH. L. REV. 551, 566 (1991) (citing barriers to entry and market power to be the two necessary conditions for exclusionary conduct).

34.   Beltone Elecs. Corp., Trade Reg. Rep. (CCH) ¶ 21,934 (FTC 1982); *see* Barry Wright Corp. v. ITT Grinnell Corp., 724 F.2d 227, 237 (1st Cir. 1987) (Breyer, J.) (considering both extent and duration of foreclosure); Roland Mach. Co. v. Dresser Indus., 749 F.2d 380, 394 (7th Cir. 1984) (Posner, J.).

35.   *LePage's*, 324 F.3d at 163 (quoting Data Gen. Corp. v. Grumman Sys. Support Corp., 36 F.3d 1147, 1183 (1st Cir. 1984)); *see also* United States v. Microsoft Corp., 253 F.3d 34, 69 (D.C. Cir. 2001). Examples of procompetitive justifications are the desire to avoid free riding by competitors on the manufacturer's providing training, customer lists, and promotional help to its retailers. *See* Dennis W. Carlton, *A General Analysis of Exclusionary Conduct and Refusal to Deal—Why* Kodak *and* Aspen *Are Misguided*, 68 ANTITRUST L.J. 659, 663 (2001).

36.   Mark S. Popofsky, *Defining Exclusionary Conduct: Section 2, the Rule of Reason, and the Unifying Principle Underlying Antitrust Rules*, 73 ANTITRUST L.J. 435, 437 (2006); Carlton, *supra* note 35, at 663 (effort to judge whether the benefits to exclusivity outweigh the anticompetitive effect); *see* 11 HOVENKAMP, *supra* note 33, ¶ 1821, at 167.

monopolize the market[37]—can dissuade a supplier from wrong-headed exclusive dealing attempts.

A variety of category management practices may provide some degree of exclusivity to the category captain. A very common arrangement will involve the supplier's payment of a promotional allowance to a retailer as consideration for advertising or displaying the product, often at a reduced price. Such an agreement might exclude other suppliers. The focus, though, will always return to the degree that competition as a whole is harmed by any given practice. Thus, any agreement to promote products usually would not be considered exclusive absent a requirement not to carry competing products.[38]

In some cases, the appointment of a category captain may be part of a marketing agreement that involves the payment of funds to a retailer by the supplier. These funds may be for specified promotional activities, such as displaying or featuring products.[39] The anticompetitive impact of requests or payments for advantageous displays traditionally has been examined to see if there were an exclusive dealing provision, and the risk of liability has tended to vary with market share and the percentage of market foreclosed by the challenged arrangement.[40] If the parties legally could have negotiated an exclusive dealing agreement, then, arguably,

---

37. *See* Conwood Co. v. U.S. Tobacco Co., 290 F.3d 768, 784–88 (6th Cir. 2002).

38. *LePage's*, 324 F.3d at 141.

39. The Clayton Act also may reach certain category management activities, to the extent they result in discounts or rebates conditioned on exclusive dealing arrangements. 15 U.S.C. § 14. Promotional allowances or services may run afoul of the Robinson-Patman Act if they are not allocated to customers on a proportionally equal basis. *See* Guides for Advertising Allowances and Other Merchandising Payments and Services, 16 C.F.R. §§ 240.1 – 240.15.

40. *See* Jefferson Parish Hosp. Dist. No. 2 v. Hyde, 466 U.S. 2, 26–29, 31 (1984) (market share of 30% did not constitute market power); Augusta News Co. v. Hudson News Co., 269 F.3d 41 (1st Cir. 2001) (paying up-front fees to chain retailers for exclusive right to supply was not per se violation of the Sherman Act); Zeller Corp. v. Fed.-Mogul Corp., No. 97-4134, 1999 U.S. App. LEXIS 6345 (6th Cir. 1999) (business lost due to failure to pay $400,000 "signing bonus"); Empire Volkswagen Inc. v. World-Wide Volkswagen Corp., 814 F.2d 90 (2d Cir. 1987) (requirement that automobile brands be sold from distinct facilities); R&G Affiliates v. Knoll Int'l, 587 F. Supp. 1395 (S.D.N.Y. 1984) (requirement that specified volume of sales be maintained in order to be allowed to carry entire line).

any promotional or category management agreement that falls short of illegal exclusive dealing also would be legal.

In *R.J. Reynolds Tobacco Co. v. Philip Morris Inc.*,[41] a competitor challenged the "Retail Leaders" promotion program used by Philip Morris, whereby a retailer could earn additional promotional funds by allowing favorable promotion and display of Philip Morris cigarettes. The plaintiffs alleged that this program monopolized and restrained trade in the U.S. cigarette market since it placed "substantial interbrand restrictions on the flow of consumer information critical to the proper functioning of a free-enterprise system."[42] Initially, an injunction was entered against portions of the program that restrained retailers from using signs for competing tobacco brands,[43] but after extensive discovery, summary judgment was entered in favor of Philip Morris. The district court, applying a rule of reason standard, determined that Philip Morris did not have market power.[44]

The plaintiffs' economist acknowledged that the promotional payments (including slotting allowances) received by participating retailers would eventually result in lower consumer prices.[45] This is an often significant point about category management programs: to the

---

41.   199 F. Supp. 2d 362 (M.D.N.C. 2002), *aff'd,* 67 F. App'x 810 (4th Cir. 2003).

42.   *Id.* at 379–80.

43.   R.J. Reynolds Tobacco Co. v. Philip Morris Inc., 60 F. Supp. 2d 502 (M.D.N.C. 1999) (order granting preliminary injunction).

44.   *R.J. Reynolds*, 199 F. Supp. 2d at 386. The district court did not think that the defendant's 51.3% market share indicated market power, given significant excess capacity, lack of supracompetitive pricing, and the success of several new brands that indicated the lack of barriers to entry. The court of appeals affirmed but did not conclude that Philip Morris lacked market power; instead, it determined that the plaintiffs failed to show that the program substantially foreclosed competition in the relevant market. *R.J. Reynolds*, 67 F. App'x at 812.

45.   *R.J. Reynolds*, 199 F. Supp. 2d at 369. The district court explained that the average prices of Philip Morris's Marlboro brand cigarettes actually declined relative to other manufacturers after the Retail Leaders promotion was implemented, and the overall level of promotional spending across the industry increased. *Id.* at 373, 379; *see also* Peter Bronsteen, Kenneth G. Elzinga & David E. Mills, *Price Competition and Slotting Allowances*, 50 ANTITRUST BULL. 267 (2005); Ramarao Desiraju, *New Product Introductions, Slotting Allowances and Retailer Discretion*, 77 J. RETAILING 335 (2001) (retailers receiving high slotting fee payments are able to offer lower consumer prices).

extent that they involve not just recommendations, but payments, discounts, or rebates to a retailer, the effect on consumer welfare should not be overlooked. The consumer benefit may be indirect where category management payments are treated as "inside margin" by the retailer, but where the payments require promotion or advertising at a reduced price, there would be a direct consumer benefit.

Another practice that could be challenged as exclusionary is a slotting allowance, which is a payment from the seller to the buyer just to get on the shelf. Many retailers insist on this kind of payment, and the economic effects are still in dispute.[46] A slotting payment may have originated as a way for retailers to receive additional compensation, but the reliance on such payments may alter the way decisions are made to carry products. Retailers are incentivized to base their decisions not just on what products will sell best, but at least in part on who will pay the greatest fee. Those two factors may coincide; the supplier of the best-selling products often has the most shelf space and can afford to pay the most for shelf access. Given that the shelf space in a store is not unlimited, any decision to take on a certain product often translates into the need to remove another product to make room for the newcomer.[47] Courts have recognized that slotting allowances can be procompetitive, reducing costs to retailers and, potentially, to consumers.[48]

In *El Aguila Food Products v. Gruma Corp.*,[49] the plaintiffs were rival suppliers complaining of defendant's use of "customer marketing agreements" and upfront payment to retailers. Through those practices, the defendant was able to obtain retail placement and displace competing products. The payments, according to the plaintiff, allowed the defendant to gain market power, and control the placement, location, availability, visibility, and promotional activity of competing retail products. El Aguila's expert testified that while the use of a slotting fee by itself was not unlawful, when combined with Gruma's category management activities, it enabled Gruma to obtain exclusivity, get

---

46.   FED. TRADE COMM'N, SLOTTING ALLOWANCES IN THE RETAIL GROCERY INDUSTRY: SELECTED CASE STUDIES IN FIVE PRODUCT CATEGORIES (2003), *available at* http://www.ftc.gov/os/2003/11/slotting allowancerpt031114.pdf.
47.   *See* Willard K. Tom, Slotting Allowances and the Antitrust Laws, Testimony before the Committee on the Judiciary, U.S. House of Representatives (1999).
48.   *Cf.* FTC v. H.J. Heinz Co., 246 F.3d 708, 719 & n.16 (D.C. Cir. 2001).
49.   301 F. Supp. 2d 612 (S.D. Tex. 2003), *aff'd*, 131 F. App'x 450 (5th Cir. 2005).

greater display space than the sales dictated, and permitted preferential space and display positions that restricted competitive promotions. Nevertheless, the evidence demonstrated that there were many private labels and other competitors present in the stores, that many new competitors had entered the market, and that the plaintiffs' tortillas were on the shelves in many of the stores where Gruma paid a slotting fee. The court thus determined that the customer marketing agreements were an "acceptable and desirable means to acquire market share,"[50] relying in part on the lack of exclusivity in the market and the refusal by some plaintiffs to offer competitive programs.[51]

2.   *Tortious Conduct Aimed at Rivals*

Section 2 has been used to attack, with mixed results, an assortment of other practices alleged to be exclusionary, including refusals to deal,[52] limiting access to essential facilities,[53] monopoly leveraging,[54] and

---

50.   *Id.* at 629.

51.   *Id.* ("[T]he evidence shows that even where [defendant] has 50% or more of the shelf space, private labels and other competitors have the remaining shelf space."). Interestingly, the Sixth Circuit focused little attention on the defendant's promotional programs in *Conwood Co. v. U.S. Tobacco Co.*, 290 F.3d 768 (6th Cir. 2002). There, although the court noted that defendant U.S. Tobacco's "Consumer Alliance Programs" involved "granting retailers a maximum discount of .3% for providing [U.S. Tobacco] with sales data, and participating in [U.S. Tobacco] promotion programs, and/or giving the best placement to [U.S. Tobacco] racks and POS," it never analyzed the programs and ultimately found the defendants liable for antitrust violations based on the commission of various business torts, such as repeatedly destroying competitors' displays and submitting deliberately misleading sales information to the retailers. *Id.* at 778.

52.   *See, e.g.*, Aspen Skiing Co. v. Aspen Highlands Skiing Corp., 472 U.S. 585, 593-94 (1985). *See generally* ABA SECTION OF ANTITRUST LAW, ANTITRUST LAW DEVELOPMENTS 258–60 (6th ed. 2007).

53.   United States v. Terminal R.R., 224 U.S. 383, 394-95 (1912); Gamco, Inc. v. Providence Fruit & Produce Bldg., 194 F.2d 484, 485-86 (1st Cir. 1952). *But see* Verizon Comm'cns v. Law Offices of Curtis V. Trinko, 540 U.S. 398, 410-11 (2004) (neither recognize nor repudiate the doctrine). *See generally* ABA SECTION OF ANTITRUST LAW, ANTITRUST LAW DEVELOPMENTS 258-66 (6th ed. 2007).

54.   *See, e.g.*, United States v. Griffith, 334 U.S. 100, 103–04 (1948). The circuit courts have been divided on what the elements of a viable

preemptive employment of needed personnel.[55]   The line between tortious conduct and antitrust violations has been ill-defined.[56]   Courts, however, are loath to permit the Sherman Act to devolve into a general prohibition of business torts. One limitation on the use of antitrust to address tortious conduct generally is the requirement of antitrust injury, that a plaintiff be injured "by reason of" a violation of the antitrust laws.[57] Applying that requirement, injury to a plaintiff that does not arise from injury to competition will not be the basis for a claim.

The *Conwood* decision[58] analyzes a variety of tortious conduct undertaken by a category captain. Although much of what was claimed there perhaps best is conceived as the province of the common law of tort, the behavior also was held to have exceeded the outer bounds of antitrust tolerance. In addition to performing usual category captain tasks, such as determining product choice and placement, U.S. Tobacco, the category captain for a number of retailers, gave misleading sales data in arguing for the discontinuation of competitive brands.[59] For example, one witness testified that the information U.S. Tobacco provided to local retailers was "skewed" to the national market, masking local movement.[60] Another witness recalled instances where the defendant "falsely reported [to retailers] that some of [its own] products were selling better than [those of its] competitors."[61] U.S. Tobacco also engaged in a pattern of outright vandalism, destroying and obscuring

---

leveraging claim would be. *See generally* ABA SECTION OF ANTITRUST LAW, ANTITRUST LAW DEVELOPMENTS 302-06 (6th ed. 2007).

55.   Taylor Pub'g Co. v. Jostens, Inc., 216 F.3d 465, 479 (5th Cir. 2000).

56.   HERBERT HOVENKAMP, THE ANTITRUST ENTERPRISE: PRINCIPLE AND EXECUTION 174–75 (2005).

57.   *See generally* Max Huffman, *A Standing Framework for Private Extraterritorial Antitrust Enforcement*, 60 SMU L. REV. 103, 106–13 (2007).

58.   Conwood Co. v. U.S. Tobacco Co., 290 F.3d 768 (6th Cir. 2002). In *Conwood*, the category captain's conduct included basic discounting to retailers and supplying promotional and sales aids, but also dumping competitors' racks and products and supplying retailers with false information about competing suppliers.

59.   *Id.* at 777.

60.   *Id.* at 776.

61.   *Id.* at 777. This assertion was supported by an internal report by a U.S. Tobacco manager: "'[W]e are not being total [sic] honest with our partners. . . . [W]e are using up our . . . good will when we . . . turn around and ask [retailers] to go against what we just convinced them was in their best interest.'" *Id.* at 786.

competitors' display racks in stores. Several of Conwood's witnesses testified that U.S. Tobacco supervisors directly ordered the destruction of Conwood's racks and that compensation and bonuses were sometimes dependent on such destruction.[62] There also were several internal documents suggesting the existence of an official U.S. Tobacco policy endorsing the elimination of competition through wrongful means.[63] U.S. Tobacco failed to provide a valid business reason for the alleged tortious conduct.[64] Its contention was that the instances of rack destruction were only "sporadic torts"[65] and that "tortious activity cannot form the basis for liability under the Sherman Act."[66] The court disagreed, holding that the conduct was exclusionary and that U.S. Tobacco maintained its monopoly power by engaging in the exclusionary conduct.[67]

---

62.   Former U.S. Tobacco employees also testified that they often dismantled Conwood sales racks, and that in some instances competitive products were hidden under a counter. *Id.* at 778–80.

63.   One memo stated that U.S. Tobacco "'would actively pursue strategies to limit the growth of the price value market segment.'" *Id.* at 776. Other memos were similarly suspect: "'it is important that [U.S. Tobacco] continue with this Category Management plan to eliminate competitive products,'" *id.* at 777; "'[w]e will continue to focus on merchandising rights to . . . inhibit competitive growth . . . to the best of our ability,'" *id.*; the "CAP 'has become a great incentive in securing space for our vendors and for the elimination of competition products.'" *Id.* at 778.

64.   *Id.* at 787.

65.   *Id.* at 783.

66.   *Id.* at 781. U.S. Tobacco further maintained that because the factual circumstances of the conduct alleged differed from store to store, the parties were required to investigate the events at each store to fully measure the extent of the tortious activity, citing *In re Airport Car Rental Antitrust Litigation*, 474 F. Supp. 1072 (N.D. Cal. 1979). The district court rejected this argument as impractical, and the appellate court agreed that "requir[ing] the parties to investigate activity at specific retail establishments would have been so costly as to have effectively ended the suit, despite substantial evidence of anti-competitive activity." *Conwood*, 290 F.3d at 784.

67.   *Id.* at 788.

Some commentators have sharply criticized the *Conwood* decision.[68] Professor Hovenkamp has argued that the tortious conduct alleged did not pose a threat of consumer harm. "[S]pread over the 300,000 stores in which the products were sold, this indicates that . . . replacement costs [for destroyed wire racks] were roughly thirty-three cents per store per month . . . . [T]hese numbers indicate that the competitive impact . . . was *de minimis*."[69] He has also argued that the degree of foreclosure accomplished in *Conwood* could not exceed 19 percent of the available retail outlets, less than the 20 percent that some consider the bare minimum to survive summary judgment.[70]

Other commentators have approved of the decision, concluding that the conduct had insufficient justification.[71]

---

68.   *Conwood* caused an increase in the attention by antitrust commentators of category management practices. *See, e.g.*, Daniel A. Crane, *Harmful Output in the Antitrust Domain: Lessons from the Tobacco Industry*, 39 GA. L. REV. 321 (2005) (discussing *Conwood* while proposing a new paradigm for antitrust law in "net-harm" industries); Richard A. Epstein, *Monopoly Dominance or Level Playing Field? The New Antitrust Paradox*, 72 U. CHI. L. REV. 49, 65 (2005) (noting that "*Conwood* . . . does not demonstrate how a demand for an exclusive agreement, independent of other illegal practices, should be treated"); Benjamin Klein, *Exclusive Dealing as Competition for Distribution 'On the Merits'*, 12 GEO. MASON L. REV. 119, 156 (2004) (arguing that exclusive dealing may be an "efficient way to contract for distributor promotional effort that maximizes the return received by distributors and, therefore, the indirect benefit received by consumers"); John E. Lopatka & William H. Page, *Economic Authority and the Limits of Expertise in Antitrust Cases*, 90 CORNELL L. REV. 617 (2005) (citing *Conwood* throughout its discussion of expert testimony in antitrust cases).

69.   HOVENKAMP, *supra* note 56, at 177.

70.   *Id.* at 177; *see also* Joshua D Wright, Antitrust Analysis of Category Management: *Conwood Co. v. United States Tobacco Co.* (George Mason Univ. Law and Econ Research Paper No. 06-38, 2006), at 27, *available at* http://ssrn.com/abstract_id=945178.

71.   Jonathan M. Jacobson, *Exclusive Dealing, "Foreclosure," and Consumer Harm*, 70 ANTITRUST L.J. 311, 361 (2002); A. Douglas Melamed, *Exclusive Dealing Arrangements and Other Exclusionary Conduct—Are There Unifying Principles?*, 73 ANTITRUST L.J. 375, 392 n.48 (2006); Stephen C. Salop, *Exclusionary Conduct, Effect on Consumers, and the Flawed Profit-Sacrifice Standard*, 73 ANTITRUST L.J. 311, 317 n.50 (2006); Gregory Werden, *The "No Economic Sense" Test for Exclusionary Conduct*, 31 J. CORP. L. 293, 301 n.64 (2006).

It is perhaps fair to assume that only where the general tortious activity is part of a pattern of exclusionary conduct will it be helpful evidence on an antitrust claim. Of course, tort remedies, including punitive damages, should also be available for destructive conduct.

Absent dirty tricks and blatantly anticompetitive behavior, category management practices can be the type of competitive conduct that antitrust law condones.[72] After all, injuries to rivals can simply be "byproducts of vigorous competition."[73] The difficulty in applying any tortious conduct standard to category captains is the uncertain line between ordinary tortious conduct and a treble-damages antitrust violation. Competitors have been maligning and elbowing out each other's products for as long as commerce has existed. Sometimes the conduct rises to the level of business defamation and tortious interference. But when does business defamation and tortious interference rise to the level of antitrust liability? How widespread does the tortious conduct need be? Can a single act be enough or does there need to be a pattern of conduct? Does a supplier acting as a category captain have some implied obligation to act more neutrally despite still being a competitor? Does a category captain retain the right to meet but not beat the competitive jabs of its competitors? These questions appear to be unresolved. And underlying this legal debate is the issue of whether any competitor's jockeying for position realistically subverts the process by which increasingly sophisticated retailers choose the products for their stores and customers.

3. Access to Competitor Information

Category captains may be given access to information concerning their competitors, thus potentially giving the captains a competitive advantage. A retailer often will know the future plans of a supplier as to price changes, promotions, and new product introductions, and it may share that information with the category captain.[74] Premature sharing of

---

72. In *El Aguila*, the court explicitly approved of the competitive use of market power: "The fact that Gruma [the defendant] is a national company, larger than the regional companies and, therefore, takes advantage of its size and finances does not establish exclusionary power." El Aguila Food Prods. v. Gruma Corp., 301 F. Supp. 2d 612, 632 (S.D. Tex. 2003), *aff'd*, 131 F. App'x 450 (5th Cir. 2005).
73. Ball Mem'l Hosp. v. Mut. Hosp. Ins., 784 F.2d 1325, 1338 (7th Cir. 1986) (Easterbrook, J.).
74. SLOTTING ALLOWANCES WORKSHOP, *supra* note 7.

this information with another supplier can allow the second supplier to match or counteract the first supplier's marketing tactics, or undercut the effectiveness of the promotion by running its own promotion at or near the same time. First mover advantages of a new product introduction can also be undermined by the retailer giving another supplier advance notice of the introduction. To the extent that these disclosures may ultimately chill future promotions or innovations, consumers may be harmed.

According to the Supreme Court in *Monsanto Co. v. Spray-Rite Services Corp.*,[75] however, "distributors are an important source of information for manufacturers."[76] Chilling the flow of information from a distributor to a manufacturer threatens an "irrational dislocation in the market."[77] The Supreme Court noted in *United States v. U.S. Gypsum Co.*[78] that sharing prices between a customer and its supplier encourages price and other types of competition among suppliers.[79] That competition among suppliers reduces prices to the retailer and, potentially, to the customer.

The bottom line is that information sharing by a retailer may be necessary to realize fully the benefits of category management, and the retailer is the only actor that knows with accuracy the actual prices charged by, and volumes purchased from, each of its suppliers. The retailer also is the most accurate and efficient source of information about the volumes sold of each product to end users and the prices charged to those consumers. That information, compiled in complete and accurate fashion, can be essential for analyzing consumer preferences and optimizing a retailer's sales and margins. Those practices are the essence of category management.

Category captains frequently base their category management recommendations on information contained in sophisticated databases, which are installed and maintained by their client retailer. Those databases track consumer purchases of each product and can generate

---

75.   465 U.S. 752 (1984).

76.   *Id.* at 763.

77.   *Id.* at 764. *Monsanto* reflects Judge Bork's wisdom that vigorous competition requires "adjustment to shifting costs and demand . . . , and it is best that appropriate responses be made as quickly as possible." ROBERT H. BORK, THE ANTITRUST PARADOX: A POLICY AT WAR WITH ITSELF 388 (1978) (expressing concerns about price rigidity under the Robinson-Patman Act).

78.   438 U.S. 422 (1978).

79.   *Id.* at 450–51 (quoting Standard Oil Co. v. FTC, 340 U.S. 231, 349-50 (1951)).

daily, weekly, monthly, quarterly, or yearly reports at the press of a button.[80] Of course, a retailer can use its own price and volume data in much the same way as a category captain does to track and predict consumer preferences and reactions to price changes and other promotional activity.[81] But the synergy of the supplier's often unique expertise and the retailer's access to essential data promises more effective category management.

The overall competitive effect of a category captain's access to information is therefore unclear and situation-dependent. No case has dealt with this issue.

But the FTC has suggested that the creation of internal firewalls within the category captain's company would eliminate competitive concerns.[82] The walls would ensure that those involved in category management do not communicate a competitor's confidential information to those involved in sales or marketing.

4. *Recommendations Made by the Category Captains*

A category captain may also be able to injure a rival through its recommendations to retailers. If the captain's recommendations result in competing products being taken partially or entirely off the shelves, or placed in unfavorable locations in the retailer's stores, the circumstance begins to look more like exclusive dealing.[83]

---

80.   The almost immediate availability of sales data for any time period could also help the retailer double-check the impartiality of the category captain's recommendations and actions, supporting former FTC Commissioner Leary's view that finding a retailer sufficiently naïve to permit its self interest to be overborne by its category captain is unlikely. *See* Thomas B. Leary, A Second Look at Category Management (May 17, 2004), http://www.ftc.gov/ speeches/leary/040519categorymgmt.pdf.

81.   A category captain may know from prior experience with other retailers which products sell best and at what prices, thereby shortening a retailer's learning curve and eliminating trial-and-error delays. Sometimes much of this information is generally known. Some retailers use a general mark-up formula to set their consumer prices, allowing anyone to calculate the wholesale price by looking at the price tag on the product. Some retailers distribute or sell their sales data to suppliers as a matter of course.

82.   SLOTTING ALLOWANCES WORKSHOP, *supra* note 7, at 51.

83.   One commentator called the captaincy relationship one of "limited exclusivity." Wright, *supra* note 70, at 2.

However, when the ultimate decision is not the subject of an agreement and remains with the retailer, courts would be less likely to find the elimination of a competitor's products to be an antitrust violation.[84]   A supplier's mere suggestion that a dealer abandon a competitor's product line is not considered exclusive dealing.[85] Similarly, when the recommendations are based on accurate and impartial data, the category captain is likely not acting in an unreasonably anticompetitive manner.

In *Conwood*,[86] although the plaintiffs were unable to name a single store that gave final approval over its snuff selection to U.S. Tobacco, the court noted that there was evidence that U.S. Tobacco, and not retailers, de facto controlled where products were placed in display racks, and did so by acting surreptitiously.[87]   U.S. Tobacco, in purposely burying Conwood's products in U.S. Tobacco racks, was found to have misrepresented the sales activity of its own products to make it appear as though they were selling better than the competition.[88]

Conversely, in *El Aguila*,[89] summary judgment was granted in favor of the category captain defendant that had made recommendations regarding competitive products.[90] Fatal to the plaintiffs' claim was their admission that the retailers had set prices, not the defendant.[91] The court found that the "fact that Gruma is a national company, larger than the regional companies and, therefore, takes advantage of its size and finances does not establish exclusionary power."[92]

---

84.   *Cf.* NicSand, Inc. v. 3M Co., 507 F.3d 442, 451–53 (6th Cir. 2007) (en banc) (no Section 2 claim stated against supplier that responded to retailers' requirements of making up-front payments and entering into multi-year supply contracts at discounted prices).

85.   *See* Stearns v. Genrad, Inc., 564 F. Supp. 1309, 1313-14 (M.D.N.C. 1983) (the statements of a distributor suggesting plaintiff stop dealing in competing lines did not constitute exclusive dealing when the plaintiff faced no sanctions for its failure to follow the suggestion), *aff'd*, 752 F.2d 942 (4th Cir. 1984).

86.   Conwood Co. v. U.S. Tobacco Co., 290 F.3d 768 (6th Cir. 2002).

87.   *Id.* at 785.

88.   *Id.* at 790.

89.   El Aguila Food Prods. v. Gruma Corp., 301 F. Supp. 2d 612 (S.D. Tex. 2003), *aff'd*, 131 F. App'x 450 (5th Cir. 2005).

90.   *Id.* at 615-16.

91.   *Id.* at 631.

92.   *Id.* at 632.

Whether recommending the elimination of a competitor's product suffices as an antitrust violation can depend on whether the recommendation results in actual exclusivity. Because courts consistently recognize that antitrust law is concerned with protecting competition and not competitors, excluding one competitor (who is, of course, the most likely plaintiff) does not mean competition is unreasonably restrained.[93] Where recommendations from a category captain are supported with accurate, localized data, and where they do not confer exclusivity on the retailer's shelves, issuing elimination recommendations is one purpose of category captains. Those recommendations can be expected to serve the captain's interest as well as the retailer's.[94]

Both the retailer and the supplier ultimately want to maximize profits. Thus, the supplier may advise the retailer on a product assortment that, arguably, will provide the retailer with greater total profits, even if the result is higher prices and lower total volume. This has been criticized as delivering no consumer benefit, since it merely maximizes profits without increasing output.[95] However, profit maximization also may be seen as the outgrowth of more effectively meeting consumers' needs, by delivering the products that they want in the way they want, and recognizing more accurately what they are willing to pay for those products. Indeed, accurately meeting consumer needs is a key driver of retailer success, and this may be reflected in

---

93. In *El Aguila*, the presence of some competitive products was enough to legitimize defendant's category management practices, even where those competing products were not plaintiffs'. *Id.* at 629; *see also* Thomas B. Leary, A Second Look at Category Management (May 17, 2004), http://www.ftc.gov/ speeches/leary/040519categorymgmt.pdf.

94. These recommendations should be the result of considering the strengths and weaknesses of all the products within one category and choosing the best among them, i.e., deciding on an interbrand instead of intrabrand basis. But as former FTC Commissioner Leary points out, "The best strategy for a captain may be to recommend a plan that will preserve its already strong market position rather than blatantly enhance it." *See* Leary, *supra* note 93; *see also* Conwood Co. v. U.S. Tobacco Co., 290 F.3d 768, 775 (6th Cir. 2002) (testimony of Kroger Co. executive about the inability of category captain to abuse its power).

95. Suman Basuroy, Murali K. Mantrala & Rockney G. Walters, *The Impact of Category Management on Retailer Prices and Performance: Theory and Evidence*, 65 J. MKTG. 16 (2001) (study of sale of detergent in 21 retail stores).

either a low price, high volume strategy, or a higher price, low volume strategy.

Arguably, retailers provide a check on practices by category captains[96] and where retailers maintain ultimate approval authority over price and category design, nonbinding recommendations by category captains are unlikely to be considered anticompetitive.[97] But if the category captain abuses its position by providing misleading or false information to the retailer, or actively engages in tortious conduct by destroying its competitors' products or marketing materials, antitrust concerns certainly will exist.[98]

5. Conclusions Regarding Exclusion Concerns

Where category management leads to an outcome such as tying or exclusive dealing, the category manager's conduct can be judged in conventional antitrust terms. Where category management is challenged in the absence of such outcomes, important countervailing considerations can come into play, such as promoting the free flow of information and the freedom of a retailer to choose how it will run its business in a highly complicated retailing environment. Care should be taken not to misjudge the process of category management just because the category captain may have market power.

---

96.   SLOTTING ALLOWANCES WORKSHOP, *supra* note 7, at 52 ("[E]xclusion of rivals by a category captain is unlikely as a practical matter: such tactics are not in the best interest of the retailer, and if a category captain behaves in that manner, it will have progressively less influence as an advisor.").

97.   A financially strong and experienced retailer might go even further and request that the category captain only comment on the retailer's plans for category management. *See, e.g.*, R. Blattberg & E. Fox, Category Management: The Category Plan, Food Marketing Institute, 1995, Guide 3, at 15 (1995) (suggesting that the retailer may rely on the supplier for information and expertise in developing category management plans); *cf. Conwood*, 290 F.3d at 775 (citing testimony of Kroger Co. executive demonstrating a category captain would be unsuccessful in attempting to monopolize through category management).

98.   *Conwood*, 290 F.3d at 768.

TABLE OF CASES

A

B

C

E

F

G

Gamco, Inc. v. Providence Fruit & Produce Building, 194 F.2d 484 (1st
Cir. 1952), 42

H

Harlem River Consumers Cooperative v. Assoc. Grocers of Harlem, Inc.,
408 F. Supp. 1251 (S.D.N.Y. 1976), 34

I

Int'l Healthcare Mgmt. v. Hawaii Coal. for Health, 332 F.3d 600 (9th
Cir. 2003), 34

J

Jefferson Parish Hospital District No. 2 v. Hyde, 466 U.S. 2 (1984), 37,
39

K

Kotteakos v. United States, 328 U.S. 750 (1946), 33

L

Lepage's Inc. v. 3M, 324 F.3d 141 (3d Cir. 2003), 37, 38, 39
Lupron Marketing & Sales Practices Litig., *In re*, 295 F. Supp. 2d 148
(D. Mass. 2003), 33

M

Masco Contractor Services E. v. Beals, 279 F. Supp. 2d 699 (E.D. Va.
2003), 34
Monsanto Co. v. Spray-Rite Service Corp., 465 U.S. 752 (1984), 29, 47

N

NicSand, Inc. v. 3M Co., 457 F.3d 534 (6th Cir. 2006), 37

R

S

T

U

V

Z

INDEX

ABA SECTION OF ANTITRUST LAW
COMMITMENT TO QUALITY

The Section of Antitrust Law is committed to the highest standards of scholarship and continuing legal education. To that end, each of our books and treatises is subjected to rigorous quality control mechanisms throughout the design, drafting, editing, and peer review processes. Each Section publication is drafted and edited by leading experts on the topics covered and then rigorously peer reviewed by the Section's Books and Treatises Committee, at least two Council members, and then other officers and experts. Because the Section's quality commitment does not stop at publication, we encourage you to provide any comments or suggestions you may have for future editions of this book or other publications.